Contents

INTRODUCTION   7

01. Fundamental Analysis 101:
An Introduction to the Art and Science of Investing   12
  What is Fundamental Analysis?   13
  Quantitative and Qualitative Fundamental Analysis   13
  How to use Fundamental Analysis   14
  The Benefits of Using Fundamental Analysis   15
  Limitations of Fundamental Analysis   16
  Key Takeaways   17

02. The ABCs of Investing:
A Beginner's Guide to Different Types of Investments   18
  The Stock Market and Stock Investments   19
    The Potential Rewards and Risks of Stock Investing   20
    Importance of Researching and Understanding a Company Before Investing in its Stock   21
  Other Types of Investments   22
    Bonds and Bond Funds   22
    Mutual Funds and ETFs   22
    Real Estate Investment Trusts (REITs)   23
    Gold and Other Precious Metals   23
    Cryptocurrencies   23
    Collectibles   23
  The Importance of a Long-Term Investment Strategy   24
    Tips and Strategies for Developing a Long-Term Investment Plan   25
  Key Takeaways   27

03. Fundamental Analysis in Action:
Investing Methods That Use Fundamental Analysis   28
  Buy-and-Hold Investing   29
  Value Investing   30
  Growth Investing   32
  Key Takeaways   35

04. The Mindset and Beliefs Behind Fundamental Analysis:
Key Considerations for Investors   36
  The Importance of Having a Long-Term Perspective   37
  The importance of Discipline and Patience   38
  Understanding Your Risk Tolerance   39
  The Role of Research and Due Diligence   40
  The Influence of Emotions and Biases   40
  The Importance of Having a Diversified Portfolio   41
  Key Takeaways   43

05. Tools of the Trade:
Essential Skills for Fundamental Analysis 44
- Research Skills: 45
- Analytical Thinking 45
- Emotional Intelligence 46
- Psychology 47
- Math and Probability 47
- Creative Thinking 48
- Basic Understanding of Economics 49
- Time Management 50
- Curiosity and a Continuous Desire to Learn 50
- Key Takeaways 52

06. Avoiding the Pitfalls:
Common Mistakes in Fundamental Analysis and How to Avoid Them 53
- Mistake 1: Relying Heavily on Past Performance 53
- Mistake 2: Failing to Diversify 54
- Mistake 3: Not Keeping up With Changes in the Market or Industry 55
- Mistake 4: Getting Caught Up in the Hype or "Herd Mentality" 55
- Mistake 5: Being too Emotional or Biased 55
- Mistake 6: Not Having a Clear Investment Plan or Strategy 56
- Mistake 7: Not Conducting Sufficient Research and Due Diligence 57
- Mistake 8: Chasing Short-Term Returns or Trying to Time the Market 57
- Mistake 9: Ignoring Risks and not Having a Plan for Managing Them 58
- Key Takeaways 59

07. The Big Picture:
Understanding a Company's Industry and Market Position 60
- Understanding a Company's Industry 61
- Industry Trends and Competitive Analysis 62
- Market Conditions and Macroeconomic Factors 64
- Analyzing a Company's Competitive Advantage 65
- Assessing Industry and Market Risks 67
- Key Takeaways 69

08. The Boss Squad:
Evaluating a Company's Management Team 70
- The Role of Management in a Company's Success 71
- How to Evaluate a Company's Management Team 72
- Common Mistakes When Evaluating Management 74
- Key Takeaways 76

09. Corporate Governance:
Making Sure a Company is run Ethically and Responsibly 77
- What is Corporate Governance? 78
- Corporate Governance Principles and Frameworks 79
- Evaluating a Company's Corporate Governance Practices 79
- Key Takeaways 82

10. Doing Good While Doing Well: The Importance of Social and
Environmental Responsibility in Investing ... 83
- The Role of Social and Environmental Responsibility in Investing ... 84
- How to Assess a Company's Social and Environmental Impact ... 85
- Investing in Socially and Environmentally Responsible Companies ... 87
- Key Takeaways ... 89

11. The Balance Sheet Blues:
Deciphering Financial Statements ... 90
- Introduction to Financial Statements ... 90
- The Balance Sheet ... 91
- The Income Statement ... 92
- The Cash Flow Statement ... 94
- Key Takeaways ... 96

12. Ratio Analysis:
Using Numbers to Evaluate a Company's Performance ... 97
- Introduction to Ratio Analysis ... 97
- Liquidity Ratios ... 98
- Profitability Ratios ... 98
- Debt Ratios ... 99
- Efficiency Ratios ... 100
- Key Takeaways ... 101

13. Peering Into the Future:
Using Financial Forecasts and Projections in Fundamental Analysis ... 102
- Introduction to Financial Forecasts and Projections ... 102
- Preparing Financial Forecasts and Projections ... 103
- Evaluating Financial Forecasts and Projections ... 105
- Key Takeaways ... 106

14. The Art of Valuation:
Different Approaches to Assessing a Company's Worth ... 107
- Introduction to Valuation ... 108
- Intrinsic Valuation ... 108
- Relative Valuation ... 109
- Discounted Cash Flow Analysis ... 110
- Key Takeaways ... 112

15. Putting it all Together:
Using Fundamental Analysis to Make Investment Decisions ... 113
- Example #1: The Coca-Cola Company ... 114
  - Step 1: Study the industry and its competitors ... 114
  - Step 2: Understand the company and its business ... 114
  - Step 3: Analyze the financials ... 115
  - Step 4: Analyze forecasts/projections ... 116
  - Step 5: Put a value on the company and check this against its stock price ... 116
- Example #2: Amazon ... 117
  - Step 1: Study the industry and competitors ... 117

Step 2: Understand the company and its business	117
Step 3: Analyze the financials	118
Step 4: Analyze forecasts/projections	120
Step 5: Put a value on the company and check this against its stock price	120
Example #3: Maruti Suzuki India Limited	121
Step 1: Study the industry and its competitors	121
Step 2: Understand the company and its business	121
Step 3: Analyze the financials	121
Step 4: Analyze forecasts/projections	122
Step 5: Put a value on the company and check this against its stock price	122
Key Takeaways	123

CONCLUSION 124
REFERENCES 126

INTRODUCTION

"An investment in knowledge pays the best interest."
— Benjamin Franklin

Perhaps you are successfully employed and working full-time. You earn a good salary, have a comfortable home, and can still save and invest each month. But despite your financial stability, you still constantly seek additional ways to generate income on the side or invest part of your income to produce even more money. It could also be that you have a long-term goal of achieving financial independence and being able to retire comfortably.

Of course, that's a fantastic idea!

In fact, if you resent the shackles of duty and responsibility to others that compel you to work for money, having alternate sources of income is the surest thing to do. It is also the easiest way to ensure financial security while providing for your family sufficiently and giving them the best opportunities in life and for their future.

So, in your quest for financial freedom, you spend most of your time on business and financial news websites and forums, such as the Wall Street Journal, the Economist, Bloomberg, etc., trying to see and learn about passive income opportunities.

Fortunately for you, you come across a post or an article that talks about investing in the capital markets to generate passive income without actively working for it. Inspired by the idea, you start researching ways to generate passive income from the capital markets, especially by trading and investing in stocks.

So you take the risk and invest a portion of your savings in the stock market. But unfortunately, your investment doesn't yield any profit. Instead, it swallows up your capital, and soon, you are scared. You see others making a living from trading and investing in the stock market, yet you don't make any headway. It even gets to the point where you now become terrified of investing in the stock market again, so you don't lose your hard-earned money.

Then you start thinking aloud…

"Will I even be free to retire early and travel the world with my family?"

"Can I truly achieve financial independence through trading and investing in stocks?"

"Perhaps, investing can ensure my financial security so that I don't ever have to worry about money again."

"OK! I really want to give investing in stocks another shot, but I don't even know how to; there's too much information that I'm scared of losing my life savings."

Of course, your questions and thoughts are valid.

A recent report about Americans' stock ownership by Gallup revealed that 58% of Americans own stocks. But while more than half the Americans own stocks, another report by NerdWallet shows that most of those who invest in the stock market don't know what stocks make up their investment portfolios. In essence, most people who invest in stocks are really gambling their money away.

As you can see, you aren't alone. Several other individuals, just like you, are facing the issue of making money from the stock market. They don't know where to start, or they've had bad experiences with lackluster investments in the past.

Regardless of whatever issue you are facing, if you value security and stability and are driven by a sense of responsibility to your career and family, I guarantee that when you read this book to the end, you will discover how you also can have a life free of financial worries and stress by investing in the stock market using fundamental analysis.

The methodologies in this book are exactly what the top gurus in the financial markets practice, which enables them to identify what stock to buy, when to buy, and when to sell and make profits.

In the end, you would be surprised at how you have improved your investing skills and well on your way to making informed decisions about your financial future.

Know that my ultimate goal is to help people like you achieve financial independence, and I've successfully done that for several years. In fact, I have been able to help people win in their personal life and career with our principled, result-oriented teaching.

My motivation for pursuing this goal is the compassionate drive to help everyone have the financial knowledge and literacy to make smart decisions with their money, so they don't have to keep working just to barely make ends meet.

And so, if you're looking for a comprehensive guide that will provide you with the necessary tools and knowledge to succeed in the stock market, look no further!

Yes, making money from the stock market can be challenging for many people, as it involves taking on risk, and there is no guarantee of returns. But the major problem is that many individuals lack a basic understanding of how the stock market works, making it difficult to make informed investment decisions.

Timing is another critical factor in the stock market, as many people find it difficult to know when to buy or sell a stock. For example, if an individual buys a stock at a high price and then the market crashes, they may lose money. And then emotional biases would set in. You start struggling with fear, greed, and hope—all of which can drive you to make impulsive investment decisions that can harm your portfolio.

Despite these challenges, we can still generate passive income from the stock market. Surprised?

Yes, we do…using the concept of fundamental analysis, a method that enables us to evaluate a stock to determine its intrinsic value. This model analyzes the financial and economic factors that can impact a company's future financial performance, including its revenue and earnings growth, financial health, and market position.

Warren Buffett, considered one of the greatest investors of all time, became successful through his use of fundamental analysis. His investment philosophy is centered around a long-term, value-oriented approach, and he relies on fundamental analysis to make informed investment decisions. He looks for companies with strong competitive advantages, such as a well-established brand, consistent earnings growth, and a healthy balance sheet, among other factors.

Other renowned investors use fundamental analysis as the basis for their investment decisions. These include Benjamin Graham, the father of value investing; Seth Klarman, the founder and CEO of The Baupost Group; Peter Lynch, a former manager of the Fidelity Magellan Fund; and David Einhorn, the founder and CEO of Greenlight Capital.

By using fundamental analysis, you can go from being a rookie in the world of stock investing to becoming a superstar in the field. By analyzing a company's financial statements, earnings, and growth potential, you will have a comprehensive view of a company's financial health. That way, you can make informed investment decisions, whether to buy the company's stocks or not.

So if you have been through the *"Oh My Goodness"* process of never feeling like you could invest in stocks again, generate passive income, get financial security, and achieve financial freedom, you may want to rethink your position.

Luckily for you, I have poured all my knowledge and experiences gained from investing in the stock market into this book, which extensively addresses fundamental analysis.

We have gone through all the pain for you so that you don't have to battle with the common enemies who are more symbolic; the "herd" mentality that collectively results in FOMO (Fear of Missing Out) on buying a stock.

"Fundamental Analysis Essentials: Master the Art of Assessing a Company's Value, Reading Financial Statements, Calculating Ratios and Setting a Buy Target" is a comprehensive guide that focuses entirely on fundamental analysis and gives a comprehensive and straightforward understanding of how you can use this form of analysis to pick promising stocks.

It reveals the step-by-step process for evaluating companies and their stocks, including studying qualitative and quantitative factors and determining how to value a company and its stocks. Outlined below are some of the specifics this book will help you achieve:

- Understanding the basics of investing and the different types of investments available;
- Gaining insight into the mindset and principles behind fundamental analysis and use it to make informed investment decisions;
- How to avoid common mistakes and fads in fundamental analysis;
- What to look for when evaluating a company's industry, including its market position, management team, corporate governance, and social and environmental responsibility;
- The different approaches to valuing a company and determining its worth as an investment;
- How to identify undervalued companies that may have strong growth potential, allowing you to potentially buy low and sell high;
- Improved long-term investment success and financial stability;
- A deeper understanding of the financial markets and how stock prices move over time;
- How to assess the risks associated with a particular stock, so you can make informed decisions about your investments and better manage your risk.

Ultimately, you will feel more confident about making investment decisions and choosing which companies to buy stocks in. You won't be as afraid about risking your money because you have a systematic approach to picking which companies to put your money in.

So, if you are looking for a way to generate passive income while you spending time with your family, travel, and participate in fun activities that help you to take your mind off work, well, you now have the solution in your hands.

Are you feeling excited already?

Well, then, let's get started!

Chapter 1

Fundamental Analysis 101: An Introduction to the Art and Science of Investing

"I will tell you how to become rich. Close the doors. Be fearful when others are greedy. Be greedy when others are fearful."
— *Warren Buffett*

This first chapter will explore fundamental analysis, why it's an important tool for investors, and its limitations. Warren Buffett, popularly referred to as the "Oracle of Omaha" and one of the most successful investors ever, swears by fundamental analysis.

In fact, Buffett became successful through his use of fundamental analysis. And till today, his investment philosophy is centered around a long-term, value-oriented approach, which heavily relies on fundamental analysis to make informed investment decisions.

Buffett's practice is to look for companies with strong competitive advantages, such as a well-established brand, consistent earnings growth, and a healthy balance sheet, among other factors.

Buffett also emphasizes understanding a company's underlying business and looking for companies he believes has a sustainable business model, as well as the potential for long-term growth. He is not swayed by short-term market fluctuations and instead focuses on the long-term financial health of a company.

In addition to using fundamental analysis, Buffett is also known for his discipline and patience as an investor. He is willing to hold onto investments for long periods and is not afraid to wait for the right opportunity to present itself.

Buffett's success as a stock investor can therefore be attributed to his use of fundamental analysis, his value-oriented approach, and his discipline and patience as an investor. By combining these elements, he has achieved remarkable returns that make other investors consider him the greatest investor of all time.

So, what exactly is this mysterious investing method, and how can it help you make better investment decisions?

Let's find out!

What is Fundamental Analysis?

Fundamental analysis evaluates the security, such as a stock or bond, to determine its intrinsic value. It is a bottom-up approach to investing that focuses on the underlying fundamentals of a company rather than external factors such as market trends or sentiment.

Fundamental analysis involves analyzing the financial and economic factors that can impact a company's future financial performance, including revenue and earnings growth, financial health, and market position.

The essence of fundamental analysis is to assess the overall financial health of a company and its future growth potential, and compare this with the current market price of its securities to determine the true value of its asset, and whether it is overvalued or undervalued relative to its intrinsic value. By doing so, fundamental analysts aim to identify potential investment opportunities and make informed investment decisions.

Fundamental analysis is unlike technical analysis, which relies on past price movements, chart patterns, and statistical analysis of market data to make predictions and identify trading opportunities. It is also different to quantitative analysis, which uses mathematical and statistical models to analyze securities. Fundamental analysis rather looks at a company's financial health, management, industry trends, and other quantitative and qualitative factors to make investment decisions.

Quantitative and Qualitative Fundamental Analysis

Fundamental analysis can be divided into two main approaches: quantitative and qualitative.

Quantitative fundamental analysis uses numerical data and financial ratios to evaluate a company's financial health and future potential. This analysis focuses on financial metrics such as earnings per share, revenue growth, debt-to-equity ratio, and return on equity.

Qualitative fundamental analysis, however, involves evaluating a company's intangible factors, such as its management quality, market position, and industry trends. This analysis includes brand recognition, customer satisfaction, and company culture.

Both types of fundamental analysis can be used together to understand a company's potential and financial health. Quantitative analysis provides a numerical representation of a company's financial performance, while qualitative analysis provides insight into the company's intangible assets and potential future growth.

How to use Fundamental Analysis

Some key components of fundamental analysis include reviewing a company's financial statements, such as its balance sheet, income statement, and cash flow statement, as well as analyzing its market position, competition, and economic environment. It also involves considering macroeconomic factors that may impact the company, such as interest rates, inflation, and economic growth.

So, let's say you want to buy Apple's stock, but you aren't sure whether it's worth it. Here's an illustration of how you would use fundamental analysis:

- **Gather financial data**: Start by gathering financial data on Apple, such as its income statement, balance sheet, and cash flow statement. You can find this information on the company's investor relations website or through financial data providers such as Yahoo Finance or Google Finance.
- **Analyze the financial statements**: Use the financial data to analyze Apple's financial performance, including its revenue growth, earnings per share, debt-to-equity ratio, and other key metrics.
- **Evaluate the company's competitive position**: Look at Apple's competitive position in the industry, including its market share, brand recognition, and product offerings.
- **Assess the company's management**: Evaluate the quality and experience of Apple's management team and the company's corporate governance practices.
- **Determine the company's intrinsic value**: Use the information gathered in the first four steps to determine Apple's intrinsic value. This can be done by estimating the future cash flows the company is expected to generate and discounting them back to the present.
- **Compare the intrinsic value to market price**: Compare the intrinsic value of Apple's stock to its current market price. If the intrinsic value exceeds the market price, the stock may be considered undervalued and a good buying opportunity.

- **Make an informed decision:** Finally, use all the information gathered in the analysis to decide whether to buy or not to buy Apple's stock.

Mind you, this is just an example and not a recommendation to buy Apple stock. It is important to thoroughly research and consider multiple factors before making investment decisions. And we will be looking into all of these factors in subsequent chapters, so just hang on.

The Benefits of Using Fundamental Analysis

Fundamental analysis is often considered the best approach for investing in the stock market for several reasons:

- **Long-term focus:** Fundamental analysis focuses on a company's financial health and stability rather than short-term market fluctuations, making it a good approach for long-term investors.
- **Informed decision-making:** By analyzing a company's financial statements, earnings, and growth potential, fundamental analysis provides a comprehensive view of a company's financial health, which can help you, as an investor, make informed investment decisions.
- **Better risk management:** Fundamental analysis helps investors assess the risks associated with a particular stock, allowing them to make informed decisions about their investments and better manage their risk.
- **Uncovering value:** Fundamental analysis helps investors identify undervalued companies with strong growth potential, allowing them to buy low and sell high.
- **Avoiding fads:** The stock market can be driven by emotions and fads, and fundamental analysis provides a more rational and evidence-based approach to investing, allowing investors to avoid costly mistakes.
- **In-depth analysis:** Fundamental analysis provides a thorough analysis of a company, including its financial statements, economic conditions, and industry trends, which can help an investor understand the overall financial health of a company.
- **Superior returns:** By investing in undervalued companies based on their fundamentals, an investor can achieve superior returns compared to the market average.

While fundamental analysis does not guarantee success in the stock market, it provides a solid foundation for informed and rational investment decisions, which can lead to better returns over the long term.

Limitations of Fundamental Analysis

Fundamental analysis, despite its benefits, also has some limitations:

- **Subjectivity:** The interpretation of financial statements and other data used in fundamental analysis can be subjective, leading to different conclusions by analysts.
- **Time lag:** Fundamental analysis typically focuses on past performance and may not be able to predict future trends accurately. It relies on the accuracy and completeness of financial statements and other data, which may not always be reliable.
- **Limited scope:** Fundamental analysis only examines a company's financial and economic indicators and may not consider other important factors, such as technological advancements, geopolitical events, market trends, or investor sentiment, which can influence the price of a security.
- **Inaccurate data:** Financial statements can be subject to manipulation, errors, or fraud, leading to inaccuracies in the data used for fundamental analysis. And that's because it requires a significant amount of time and effort to analyze a company's fundamentals properly.
- **Market movements:** Fundamental analysis may not be suitable for all investments, such as highly volatile or illiquid assets. It also does not always align with market movements, as market sentiment can be driven by factors other than a company's financial health.
- **Limited scope of analysis:** Fundamental analysis may not be suitable for companies operating in emerging markets or industries with limited financial data and information.

Notwithstanding, fundamental analysis is a comprehensive and evidence-based approach to investing that considers both short-term and long-term factors to determine a security's intrinsic value. It is one of the tools you must have in your investment strategy arsenal.

Now that we have a foundational understanding of fundamental analysis, we will delve into the basics of investing, including different types of investments and the risks and rewards associated with each.

Key Takeaways

- Buffett's success as a stock investor can be attributed to his use of fundamental analysis, value-oriented approach, and discipline and patience.

- Fundamental analysis is a bottom-up approach to investing that focuses on the underlying fundamentals of a company rather than external factors such as market trends or sentiment.

- Fundamental analysis can be divided into two main approaches: quantitative and qualitative.

- Some key components of fundamental analysis include reviewing a company's financial statements, such as its balance sheet, income statement, and cash flow statement.

- Fundamental analysis provides a great view of a company's financial condition.

Chapter 2
The ABCs of Investing: A Beginner's Guide to Different Types of Investments

"The stock market is filled with individuals who know the price of everything, but the value of nothing."
— Phillip Fisher

When it comes to investing, the saying 'don't put all your eggs in one basket' couldn't be truer, especially regarding the diversification of one's investments.

This phrase originates from a tale about a farmer who had a basket of eggs and was carrying it to market to sell. Along the way, he stumbled, and the basket fell, breaking all the eggs.

The farmer learned from the bitter experience as he knew that it was foolish to put all of his eggs in one basket.

So, he decided to distribute the eggs between more baskets so that if he lost one basket, he still had eggs to sell.

When we apply this context to investing, it simply means it's wise to spread your money across various investments instead of putting all your money into one stock or one type of investment.

That means if one investment doesn't perform well, your overall portfolio will still have a chance to perform well instead of being entirely at risk. Diversification helps to reduce the risk of losing money, and it's a key principle in building a successful long-term investment strategy.

But creating a diverse investment portfolio right for you isn't always easy. And that's why in this chapter, we want to explore the basics of investing, including the different types of investments available, the risks and rewards of different investments, and the importance of diversification. This way, you can find out what investment strategy works for you.

The Stock Market and Stock Investments

So, first, let's talk about the stock market, its basics, and how it works.

A stock market is a place where you can buy and sell ownership in public companies (known as "stocks" or "shares"). When you buy a stock, you become a partial company owner, and the purchased shares represent your ownership.

The stock market also makes it possible for companies to raise capital by selling shares to the public while enabling people to invest their money in the hopes of earning a profit.

There are different types of stocks, each with unique characteristics, risks, and potential rewards, offered by companies to the public. These include:

- **Common stock:** This is the most common type of stock representing ownership in a company. As a common stockholder, you have the right to vote on important company matters, such as electing board members, and you also receive dividends if the company declares them. The potential reward is that the value of the stock can increase over time, leading to capital gains. But there is also the risk that the stock value can decrease, leading to capital losses.

- **Preferred stock**: Unlike common stock, preferred stock has a higher claim on assets and earnings. As a preferred stockholder, you receive dividends at a fixed rate and are paid before common stockholders. While preferred stock generally has less potential for capital gains than common stock, it is considered less risky.

- **Value stock:** These are shares in companies considered undervalued compared to their counterparts. In this case, a company may have an underperforming history, but it may also have strong financials and a solid track record. As an investor, buying value stocks may offer the potential for capital gains should the market recognize their true value. But there is also the risk that a value stock may underperform if the market fails to recognize its value.

- **Growth stock**: Growth stocks are shares in companies expected to grow faster than the overall market. These companies often reinvest their earnings into their business to fuel future growth rather than paying dividends to shareholders. And so they offer the potential for higher returns and are more volatile.

- **Penny stock**: This type of stock is usually priced at less than $5 per share. They are considered low-priced and high-risk investments, as smaller, less established companies often issue them with limited track records. While the low price of penny stocks can make them appealing to investors—as they may seem like a low-cost way to get into the stock market—it's important to understand that the low price of these stocks is often a reflection of their limited financial resources and uncertain future.

As a result, penny stocks can be highly speculative and volatile, and their value can fluctuate greatly quickly. In addition, penny stocks are often subject to manipulation, with unscrupulous individuals using tactics such as "pump and dump" schemes to artificially inflate the stock's price. Once the price has been inflated, the individuals behind the scheme sell their shares, causing the stock's price to plummet and leaving other investors holding the bag. So, it's generally not recommended for the average investor to invest in penny stocks but in more established companies with a proven track record and solid financials.

Meanwhile, we've got the stock exchanges and stock brokers who play an important role in the functioning of the stock market.

A stock exchange is a platform where stocks, bonds, and other securities are traded between buyers and sellers. It provides a centralized location for trading securities, ensuring transparency and fairness in the market. The major stock exchanges around the world include the New York Stock Exchange (NYSE), the London Stock Exchange (LSE), and the Tokyo Stock Exchange (TSE).

On the other hand, stockbrokers are intermediaries connecting investors to the stock market. They act as intermediaries between buyers and sellers of securities, executing trades on behalf of their clients. Some provide investors various services, including research and analysis, investment advice, and trading facilities. Stock brokers can be individuals or firms, and they typically earn a commission for each trade they execute on behalf of their clients.

In addition, there is an important concept every investor must pay attention to when investing in the stock market: diversification. By diversifying a stock portfolio, you can reduce the overall risk of your investments and improve your chances of achieving your long-term financial goals. Chapter 4 will examine the key reasons diversification is important in a stock portfolio.

The Potential Rewards and Risks of Stock Investing

Of course, while stock investing can offer the potential for substantial rewards, it also comes with several risks that investors should be aware of. Here are some of the key potential rewards and risks associated with stock investing:

Potential rewards:

- The value of a stock can increase over time, resulting in capital appreciation and a profit for you as the investor.
- As I explained earlier, many companies pay dividends to their shareholders, providing an additional source of income for the investor.
- Investing in stocks also helps investors to diversify their investment portfolio, reducing the overall risk and improving the chances of success.

Risks:

- The stock market is subject to fluctuations due to various economic, political, and market factors. And this can result in fluctuations in the value of individual stocks and the overall market.
- The performance of a company and its stock can also be impacted by certain factors, including changes in management, competition, market conditions, and even financial difficulties. And when any of these issues occur, it can lead to a decline in the stock value, causing a loss for the investor.

Importance of Researching and Understanding a Company Before Investing in its Stock

Researching and understanding a company before investing in its stock is a critical step every wise investor should take to make informed investment decisions.

For instance, researching a company's financial statements, management, and operations can provide you with valuable insights into the company's financial health and prospects. This information can help you assess the company's ability to generate profits and grow its business and potential for future success.

Understanding a company's strengths and weaknesses, competitive position, and future growth prospects can help you make informed investment decisions. This information can also help you assess the company's risk profile and determine whether its stock fits your investment goals and risk tolerance.

By researching a company, you can also become aware of potential risks, such as declining sales, weak financial performance, or regulatory issues. This information can help you decide whether to buy the company's stock or adjust your portfolios accordingly.

In essence, researching a company before buying its stock puts you in a better position to identify if it has strong growth prospects, which can result in higher returns on your investment over the long term.

Other Types of Investments

Investing in stocks and other types of investments can be a good way to grow your wealth over time. But you can consider other types of investments, each with its advantages and risks. Some of the most common types of investments include:

Bonds and Bond Funds

Bonds are debt securities that corporations, municipalities, and government entities issue. When an investor buys a bond, they essentially lend money to the issuer in exchange for periodic interest payments and the return of the principal at maturity. Bond funds are portfolios of bonds that investment professionals manage.

The potential rewards of investing in bonds and bond funds include regular income through interest payments and potential capital appreciation if the bond is sold at a premium to its face value. Bond funds also offer the potential for diversification and professional management.

Meanwhile, the risks associated with bonds and bond funds include credit risk (the risk that the issuer will default on its interest payments or principal), interest rate risk (the risk that changes in interest rates will impact the value of the bond), and inflation risk (the risk that the value of the bond will be eroded by inflation).

Mutual Funds and ETFs

Mutual funds are portfolios of securities that investment professionals manage. ETFs (exchange-traded funds) are similar to mutual funds but are traded like stocks on an exchange.

The potential rewards of investing in mutual funds and ETFs include diversifying, managing your investment professionally and exposing your portfolio to various asset classes.

But there are risks associated with mutual funds and ETFs too. These include market risk (the risk that the value of the securities in the fund will decline), management risk (the risk that the fund's manager will make poor investment decisions), and the risk of poor performance relative to the market or a benchmark.

Real Estate Investment Trusts (REITs)

REITs own, operate, or finance income-producing real estate properties. REITs offer investors the opportunity to invest in real estate without the hassle of directly owning and managing property.

The rewards of investing in REITs include the potential for steady income through dividends, exposure to real estate as an asset class, and capital appreciation if the REITs' properties increase in value.

Meanwhile, there are risks too, and these include real estate market risk (the risk that the value of the properties owned by the REIT will decline), interest rate risk (the risk that changes in interest rates will impact the value of the REIT), and the risk of poor performance relative to the market or a benchmark.

Gold and Other Precious Metals

Gold and other precious metals are often considered a hedge against inflation and market volatility. Investors can purchase physical gold or invest in gold-backed securities such as exchange-traded funds (ETFs) or mutual funds.

Investing in gold and other precious metals offers the investor the potential for price appreciation if the price of the metal increases and the potential for diversification and portfolio stability as a hedge against inflation and market volatility.

But you may experience price volatility, the risk of theft or loss, and the risk that the metal's price will decline if demand for the precious metal decreases.

Cryptocurrencies

Cryptocurrencies are digital or virtual tokens that use cryptography to secure and verify transactions, with Bitcoin being the most popular cryptocurrency.

Investing in cryptocurrencies offers high returns if the cryptocurrency's price appreciates and the potential for diversification and portfolio stability as a hedge against inflation and market volatility.

But the high price volatility, the risk of fraud or hacking, and the lack of government regulation make investing in the cryptocurrency market risky.

Collectibles

Collectibles, which may include different forms of art, stamps, NFTs (non-fungible tokens), etc., are another interesting investment option for investors to consider, especially those who enjoy collecting items with personal significance or emotional value.

If you invest in a collectible item that becomes more valuable over time, you can see a significant return on your investment. Investing in collectibles also enables you to diversify your investment portfolio and reduce overall risk.

But unlike stocks or bonds, it may not be challenging to sell collectibles quickly if you need the money. The market for a particular collectible item may be limited, making it hard to find a buyer and get the price you want.

In addition, collectible items often require careful storage and maintenance to preserve their value. And this can be expensive and may impact your overall return on investment.

The Importance of a Long-Term Investment Strategy

In investing, taking a long-term approach is the key to winning the game and reaching your financial goals over the long term. By taking a long-term investment approach, you can benefit from the power of compounding, diversification, and the tendency of the stock market to rise over time.

Historically, if you align your portfolio for the long run, you have a better chance of making money. Stocks have a roughly 50-50 chance of rising or decreasing, but they can only fall to zero and climb indefinitely. If you let your winners run, there's a significant probability that your portfolio will expand in value over time, especially if you focus on high-quality businesses.

Meanwhile, time is an important factor for playing it long-term in the stock market as it enables you to study trends and patterns carefully to reduce risk. You can make informed decisions about your investments by analyzing the historical performance of a stock or the market as a whole. For example, if a stock has consistently performed well over a long period, it will likely continue to perform well in the future, making it a safer investment. On the other hand, a stock with a history of volatility or underperformance may be riskier. This means that the longer you hold an investment, the more time it has to grow and appreciate potentially.

In addition, time allows for mitigating short-term market fluctuations and emotions. Rather than making hasty decisions based on short-term market movements, you can take a long-term view and focus on the big picture. Short-term market fluctuations can be volatile and unpredictable, so a long-term approach helps to smooth out these fluctuations and reduce the risk of making poor investment decisions.

However, trying to time the market has potential drawbacks because it can be difficult and requires a high level of skill and knowledge, especially when chasing short-term returns or attempting to buy into investments that have recently performed well. Doing so will often lead to impulsive and emotional decision-making, which can be detrimental to long-term success. And this is because the stock market is influenced by a wide range of factors, including economic conditions, company performance, and global events.

Dollar-cost averaging and reinvesting dividends are other important strategies that play an important role in long-term investment as they can help to reduce risk and increase long-term wealth.

Dollar-cost averaging involves investing a fixed amount of money at regular intervals, regardless of the price, rather than trying to time the market. This approach smooths out the impact of market fluctuations, reducing the risk of being at the top of the market, and can also take advantage of dips in the market. Over time, this approach can result in a lower average cost per investment and increase overall returns.

Reinvesting dividends is a strategy that allows investors to compound the returns received from their investments and use them to purchase additional shares of the same investment. This allows the investor to steadily accumulate more shares over time and benefit from the compounding effect of their investments. Additionally, reinvesting dividends can provide a reliable source of income and help to reduce the risk of the portfolio by diversifying the types of investments.

Tips and Strategies for Developing a Long-Term Investment Plan

When developing a long-term investment strategy, your financial goals and risk tolerance plays a critical role. Understanding your financial goals and risk tolerance helps you determine the type of investments appropriate for you and create a well-diversified and balanced portfolio that aligns with your investment objectives.

Financial goals help to define your investment priorities and provide a roadmap for your investment strategy. For example, if your goal is to save for retirement, you may want to focus on investments that offers long-term growth and stability. On the other hand, if you have a short-term goal, such as saving for a down payment on a house, you may need to prioritize investments with higher liquidity.

Risk tolerance, on the other hand, is a measure of an investor's willingness and ability to tolerate the ups and downs of the market. Investors with a high-risk tolerance may be more comfortable with investments that have the potential for high returns but also higher volatility. In comparison, investors with a low-risk tolerance may prefer more conservative investments that offer lower returns but also lower volatility. (We will talk more about risk tolerance in Chapter 4.)

Once you can identify your financial goals and define your risk tolerance, you can develop a long-term investing strategy.

You can invest in a mix of asset classes, such as stocks, bonds, and cash. And, of course, you want to consider diversifying within asset classes, such as owning stocks of companies across different sectors and industries. And if any investment in your portfolio is underperforming or losing value, there is no shame in admitting mistakes and selling assets to avoid additional loss.

It is also important to periodically review and rebalance your portfolio to ensure it remains diversified and aligned with your goals.

Never believe a stock tip, regardless of its source. Before investing your money, always conduct your research on a firm. Tips occasionally work, depending on the source's legitimacy, but long-term success necessitates extensive research.

Finally, do your best to stick to a strategy once you have a strategy. There are numerous approaches to stock selection, and it is critical to adhere to a single philosophy. Changing your strategy often turns you into a market timer, which is dangerous ground. Consider how famed investor Warren Buffett kept to his value-oriented strategy, which helped him to avoid the late-'90s dotcom boom, averting big losses when tech businesses imploded.

In the end, developing a long-term investment strategy requires you to understand the stock market and how it works, know the different types of investment, and carefully consider your financial goals, risk tolerance, and investment time horizon. It's important to understand the characteristics of each type of stock and how they fit into your overall investment strategy.

Now that we have a solid understanding of the basics of investing, we will advance our study by examining the different methods of investing that utilize fundamental analysis to make informed decisions in the next chapter.

Key Takeaways

- A stock market is a place where you can buy and sell ownership in public companies (known as "stocks" or "shares").
- Investing in stocks and other types of investments can be a good way to grow your wealth over time.
- In investing, taking a long-term approach is the key to winning the game and reaching your financial goals over the long term.

Chapter 3

Fundamental Analysis in Action: Investing Methods That Use Fundamental Analysis

"I don't look to jump over seven-foot bars; I look around for one-foot bars that I can step over."
— *Warren Buffett*

Imagine that you're in a crowded market and see two fruit stalls. One of them sells ripe and juicy apples at a discounted price, while the other sells rare and exotic fruits in high demand but at a premium price.

As a value investor, you would opt for the first stall and buy the discounted apples. You believe the apples are undervalued and the market will eventually recognize their true worth, resulting in a higher price and a good return on your investment.

On the other hand, as a growth investor, you would opt for the second stall and buy rare and exotic fruits. You believe that the fruits have a high growth potential and that their demand and price will continue to rise, resulting in a good return on your investment.

In investing, value investing is similar to buying undervalued stocks that are expected to increase in value. In contrast, growth investing is similar to buying stocks with high growth potential and increased earnings in the future. Both approaches can effectively achieve good returns, but it ultimately depends on the investor's goals, risk tolerance, and investment strategy.

Different approaches are based solely on fundamental analysis that investors can use to invest in the stock market. But this chapter focuses on the major three: buy-and-hold, value, and growth investing.

Do you want to know the difference between these three methods and which is right for you?

Then join me as we look into the key considerations for each approach, including examples of how to use them.

Buy-and-Hold Investing

Buy-and-hold investing is a long-term investment strategy that involves buying stocks or other assets and holding onto them for some time, typically several years or more. The goal of buy-and-hold investing is to benefit from the potential appreciation of the assets over time, the dividends, or other income they may generate and to reduce market timing risk by avoiding the need to constantly buy and sell securities in response to short-term market fluctuations.

This strategy involves a passive approach to investing, where the investor is not actively buying and selling assets but rather holding onto them for the long term.

For example, let's say an investor decides to buy 100 shares of company stock at $50 per share. The total investment would be $5,000. The investor then decides to hold onto the stock for several years, during which time the stock price fluctuates but eventually grows to $70 per share. At this point, the investor decides to sell their shares, which would now be worth $7,000, for a profit of $2,000.

In this example, the investor didn't attempt to time the market or make any short-term trades, but instead held onto their investment for an extended period. This is the essence of the buy and hold strategy: the belief that the stock market will grow over the long term, and so an investor's stocks will also grow in value.

By following a buy-and-hold investment strategy, you can take advantage of the power of compounding over time and potentially achieve good returns on your investments over the long term. While buy-and-hold investing requires a long-term commitment, it's important to periodically monitor your portfolio and rebalance it as needed to ensure that your investments remain aligned with your goals and risk tolerance.

Here are some benefits and drawbacks of buy-and-hold investing:

Benefits:
- **The power of compounding**: Buy-and-hold investing takes advantage of compounding, which is the ability of investments to grow over time due to reinvested earnings.
- **Long-term growth potential**: You'll also be able to take advantage of the long-term growth potential of well-established companies
- **Lower stress**: By avoiding the need to monitor the market and make short-term investment decisions constantly, buy-and-hold investing can help to reduce stress, provide a sense of stability and predictability, and increase

peace of mind since you are not constantly trading in and out of different assets.

Drawbacks:

- **Market risk**: It involves a certain level of market risk. As the assets are held longer, long-term investments can be impacted by market fluctuations or economic downturns.

- **Inactivity**: By holding onto investments over the long term, buy-and-hold investors may miss out on potential short-term gains or new investment opportunities. It can also result in a permanent loss of capital if the assets decline in value.

- **Lack of flexibility**: Buy-and-hold investing requires a long-term investment horizon and may not be suitable for investors with shorter investment goals or changing financial needs.

The buy-and-hold strategy best suits investors with a long-term investment horizon, a well-diversified portfolio, and a relatively low-risk tolerance. This type of investor is willing to weather short-term market fluctuations and is focused on achieving long-term investment goals, such as retirement or building wealth over time. So this strategy may also appeal to you if you strongly believe in the market's long-term growth potential.

Of course, there are no guarantees in the stock market, and the value of a stock can also decrease over time, which is why it's important to thoroughly research and consider a company's financial health and prospects before investing.

Value Investing

Value investing is a long-term investment strategy that involves identifying and buying undervalued assets with the expectation that the market will eventually recognize their value.

As a value investor, you typically look for assets trading at a discount to their intrinsic value, which can be determined through fundamental analysis, such as analyzing a company's financial statements, management team, and industry position.

The goal of value investing aims to identify companies with strong financial fundamentals that the market has overlooked, then buy their undervalued assets and sell them when their value has been realized to generate above-average returns.

So, for example, say there is a company named ABC Inc. that operates in the food and beverage industry. The company's earnings per share (EPS) for the past five years have been consistently high, and its financials are solid. After thoroughly analyzing the company and the industry, an investor determines that ABC Inc. is worth $100 per share based on its future earnings potential and assets. However, the stock's current market price is only $80 per share.

A value investor sees this as an opportunity to purchase ABC Inc. stock at a discount to its intrinsic value. They believe the market will eventually recognize the company's true value, and the stock price will rise to reflect it. The investor buys a large number of shares of ABC Inc. at $80 per share and holds onto them, waiting for the market to catch up.

A few months later, the market started recognizing the true value of ABC Inc., and the stock price began to rise. As more investors become aware of the company's strong financials and good future earnings potential, the demand for the stock increases, pushing the price up. The value investor who bought the stock at $80 per share now sees their investment increase in value, and they can sell their shares for a profit.

In this example, the value investor used a disciplined and systematic approach to identify undervalued securities and then purchased them at a discount. By doing so, they could generate a profit by taking advantage of the mispricing in the market. This is the basic principle of value investing.

Value investing is considered a long-term investment strategy, as it may take several years for the market to recognize a company's true value. However, it can be a rewarding strategy for patient and disciplined investors.

Here are some benefits and drawbacks of value investing:

Benefits:

- **Margin of safety**: It can provide a margin of safety, as investors buy assets at a discount to their intrinsic value.

- **Potential for higher returns**: Value investing is often associated with higher returns, as investors seek companies that the market has overlooked and have the potential for substantial growth.

- **Strong financial fundamentals**: Value investors focus on companies with strong financial fundamentals, such as solid revenue growth, low debt levels, and stable earnings. These companies are often better positioned to weather market downturns and may provide more stability to an investment portfolio. And so, this type of strategy may be suitable for investors who are more risk-averse or have a lower tolerance for volatility.

Fundamental Analysis Essentials

Drawbacks:

- **Timing risk:** Timing the market can be difficult, and it may take several years to recognize the value of an undervalued company. Analyzing a company's fundamentals properly also requires significant time and effort.

- **Limited upside potential:** While value investing can provide the potential for higher returns, there is also the risk that the market may never recognize the value of an undervalued company. That is, they may be vulnerable to the risk that the assets remain undervalued or decline in value.

- **Active management:** Value investing requires active management, as investors must continually research and evaluate companies to identify undervalued ones. This can be time-consuming and may not be suitable for all investors, especially those who need to access their money in the short term.

In the long run, the value investing strategy typically suits long-term, patient investors willing to conduct in-depth research on potential investments and are comfortable with a higher level of market risk. It may appeal to more analytical investors who strongly believe in the power of fundamental analysis to identify undervalued assets.

Value investors are often seeking to build a diversified portfolio of stocks with the potential for substantial growth over the long term. They typically have a low tolerance for short-term market fluctuations and are more focused on identifying companies with strong financial fundamentals and a sustainable competitive advantage.

Value investors are often willing to take a contrarian approach and go against the prevailing market trend to identify undervalued companies. They may also be willing to hold onto their investments for several years, even if the market is not immediately recognizing the value of their investments.

Growth Investing

Growth investing is an investment strategy that focuses on identifying and buying stocks in companies expected to experience rapid and substantial growth in the future. This growth can come from factors such as expanding market share, new product or service offerings, or improving financial performance.

Growth investors look for companies with high earnings growth potential and a strong track record of profitability. They are often willing to pay a premium for these growth opportunities and are less concerned about the current price of a stock relative to its earnings or assets.

Growth investors typically focus on younger, fast-growing companies in technology, biotechnology, and consumer goods. These companies often reinvest a significant portion of their earnings into the business to fuel future growth rather than paying dividends to shareholders.

Suppose you identify a company that sells a unique product, has a strong management team, and has shown consistent revenue growth over the past few years. You believe the company's earnings will continue to grow due to its innovative product and market position.

You decide to invest $10,000 into the company's stock. Over the next year, the company's earnings grew by 20%, and its stock price increased by 30%. Your investment of $10,000 is now worth $13,000.

You hold onto the stock for another year, the company's earnings grow by another 15%, and its stock price increases by 25%. Your investment is now worth $16,375.

In this example, you have realized gains from the company's growth and stock price appreciation. As a growth investor, you focus on buying stocks of companies with strong earnings potential and holding onto those stocks for the long term to realize gains as the companies grow.

In essence, growth investing is to generate high returns over the long term by investing in companies that are expected to grow rapidly. The focus is on capital appreciation, as opposed to income generation.

Here are some benefits and drawbacks of growth investing:

Benefits:

- **Potential for high returns**: Growth investing can generate substantial returns over the long term, as the focus is on investing in companies with strong growth potential.

- **Capital appreciation**: Growth investors are primarily focused on capital appreciation, as opposed to income generation, which means that the value of their investments can increase significantly over time.

- **Exposure to innovative companies**: Growth investing provides investors with opportunity and exposure to innovative and fast-growing companies with strong growth potential that the market may not yet recognize. And this can be a great way to capitalize on technological and market trends.

Drawbacks:

- **High risk**: Growth investing is often associated with a high level of risk, as the companies in which growth investors invest may be unproven and may not perform as expected.

- **Volatility**: Growth stocks are often more volatile than other types of stocks, which means that the value of a growth portfolio can fluctuate significantly over short periods.

- **Lack of income:** Growth companies often reinvest a significant portion of their earnings into the business to fuel future growth rather than paying dividends to shareholders. This means that growth investors may not receive income from their investments.

- **Lack of predictability**: Predicting a company's future success is difficult, and growth investors must be able to accurately identify companies with strong growth potential to achieve the desired returns.

The growth investing strategy is best suited for investors with a high-risk tolerance, a long-term investment horizon, and those seeking to generate high returns. It is typically most appropriate for young or aggressive investors willing to take on more risk to achieve higher returns.

This strategy may appeal to investors more focused on short-term or intermediate-term gains and willing to be more active in buying and selling assets. It may also be a good fit for investors who have a strong belief in the long-term growth potential of certain companies or sectors.

Growth investors are often willing to pay a premium for high-quality growth stocks and are less concerned about the current price of a stock relative to its earnings or assets. They are often interested in innovative companies in fast-growing industries, such as technology, biotechnology, and consumer goods.

Additionally, growth investing may be a good strategy for investors who are not relying on their investments for immediate income. Growth companies often reinvest a significant portion of their earnings back into the business to fuel future growth rather than paying dividends to shareholders.

It is important to note that growth investing is not suitable for all investors, as the high risk associated with this strategy may not be appropriate for everyone. Before implementing a growth investing strategy, it is important to carefully consider your investment goals, risk tolerance, and overall financial situation.

In conclusion, by analyzing a company's financials, market position, and growth prospects, the fundamental analysis provides a comprehensive picture of a company's intrinsic value and potential as an investment opportunity.

The next chapter will delve deeper into the principles behind fundamental analysis and the key considerations investors should consider when utilizing this approach.

Key Takeaways

- Buy-and-hold investing involves a passive approach to investing, where the investor is not actively buying and selling assets but rather holding onto them for the long term.

- Value investing is a long-term investment strategy that involves identifying and buying undervalued assets with the expectation that the market will eventually recognize their value.

- Growth investors look for companies with high earnings growth potential and a strong track record of profitability.

Chapter 4
The Mindset and Beliefs Behind Fundamental Analysis: Key Considerations for Investors

"Courage taught me no matter how bad a crisis gets ... any sound investment will eventually pay off."
— Carlos Slim Helu

Hailey is a well-known seasoned investor renowned for her success in the stock market. People often ask her what her secret is, and she always replies with a smile, "I believe in the power of fundamental analysis." Hailey firmly believes that a company's true value can be found in its financial statements and other fundamental data. She spends hours every week reviewing balance sheets, income statements, and cash flow statements and tracking economic indicators and market trends.

One day, a friend asked her why she focused on this approach instead of following the latest market trends or hot stocks. Hailey explained that she felt that by focusing on the fundamentals, she could identify companies with strong growth potential and long-term stability. She also shared that by studying a company's financial statements and understanding its business operations, she could make more informed investment decisions and avoid the risk of being caught up in market hype or short-term fluctuations.

Her friend was intrigued by her approach and decided to try fundamental analysis. After a few months, he was impressed by the results and realized that Hailey was right. By focusing on the fundamentals, he made more informed investment decisions and achieved greater success in the stock market.

Hailey's story highlights the mindset and beliefs behind fundamental analysis, which emphasizes the importance of understanding a company's financial statements and business operations to make informed investment decisions. This chapter will delve into the beliefs and values essential for successful fundamental analysis investing, including the mindset and approach needed to perform fundamental analysis and the specific skills and knowledge required.

The Importance of Having a Long-Term Perspective

Having a long-term perspective can help you, as an investor, to avoid being swayed by short-term market fluctuations or noise. You can take a more measured and rational investment approach rather than being swayed by emotions or biases. A long-term perspective can also help you focus on a company's fundamental strengths and potential rather than being distracted by short-term performance. The benefits of having a long-term perspective as a fundamental analysis investor include the following:

- **Time horizon**: Companies are generally evaluated based on their long-term prospects, not just short-term results. Fundamental investors can better assess a company's underlying health and potential by taking a long-term view.

- **Volatility reduction**: Stock prices can be volatile in the short term due to market events or emotional market movements, but these fluctuations tend to smooth out over time. Investing with a long-term perspective can reduce the impact of short-term volatility on your portfolio.

- **Compound growth**: Investing for the long term allows compound growth's power to work in your favor. By holding investments for an extended period, you can take advantage of the compounding of returns, leading to significant growth in your portfolio over time.

- **Reduced trading costs**: By taking a long-term view, an investor can reduce the frequency of buying and selling, lowering trading costs and increasing the return on investment.

- **Reduced emotional bias**: It is often difficult for investors to remain rational in the face of short-term market volatility. An investor can reduce the emotional bias that often leads to poor investment decisions by taking a long-term view.

- **Tax benefits**: A long-term perspective can also be beneficial for tax purposes, as it allows investors to hold onto assets for longer periods, potentially qualifying for long-term capital gains rates.

Imagine you've got a long-term perspective and are saving for your retirement. You've been following the stock market for years and noticed that tech stocks have performed well in recent years. Despite this, you decide not to invest heavily in tech stocks because you understand that the stock market is cyclical and may not perform as well in the future. Instead, you diversify your portfolio by investing in a mix of stocks, bonds, and mutual funds.

One day, you hear on the news that tech stocks have taken a sharp dip due to a new competitor entering the market. Many of your friends are selling their tech stock holdings, but you decide to stay invested. You know the market has historically recovered from short-term fluctuations over the long term, and you are confident in the fundamentals of the tech companies you have invested in.

A few months later, the tech market recovers, and your tech stock holdings have increased in value. Meanwhile, your friends who sold their tech stock holdings regret their decision, as they missed out on the market rebound.

This illustration demonstrates how a long-term perspective can help an investor make more measured and rational investment decisions, even in the face of market volatility.

By focusing on the fundamentals and maintaining a diversified portfolio, you can weather the short-term market downturn and ultimately achieve better results over the long term.

The importance of Discipline and Patience

Discipline is important because it helps investors stick to their investment strategy and not be swayed by emotions even when market conditions are unfavorable. Fundamental analysis is a long-term approach to investing, and it can take time to see the results of your research. Without discipline, abandoning your strategy and making impulsive decisions based on short-term market movements can be tempting.

Patience is also important, as it allows investors to wait for the right opportunities to present themselves and not feel pressure to make hasty decisions. It is important to wait for the right opportunities and not be swayed by short-term market noise. The focus should be on a company's long-term prospects, which requires patience and the ability to look beyond the current market conditions.

Here are some tips for staying disciplined and patient as an investor:

- **Pay yourself first**: if you aren't disciplined enough to carve off a portion of your monthly income for savings and investments, you can't realize the benefits that also come from the second and third principles of sound investing.
- **Put time on your side**: If you get into the habit of setting aside a portion of your income early, you can reap the impact that time has on investing through the power of compounding.

- **Stay informed, but avoid overreacting to news**: Stay informed about market conditions and trends, but don't let short-term news and events drive your investment decisions. Remember that the stock market is inherently volatile in the short term and that the long-term historical trend has been upward.
- **Invest regularly**: When investing a set amount at regular intervals over several years, you buy shares of your investment through up and down market cycles. The fixed amount you invest monthly will buy more shares when prices are down and fewer when prices are up. One method you can use to achieve this goal is dollar-cost averaging.

Both discipline and patience are key to the success of fundamental analysis investing. By maintaining a systematic and long-term approach, investors can make informed decisions and potentially realize higher returns in the future. These qualities can also help investors avoid trying to time the market or chasing short-term returns.

Understanding Your Risk Tolerance

Tom has a low-risk tolerance and is looking for steady, consistent investment returns. He invests mainly in bonds and high-quality blue-chip stocks, which are known for their stability and reliability.

One day, Tom's friend, an investment advisor, tells him about a new cryptocurrency that has been gaining popularity and has the potential for high returns. Despite his friend's enthusiasm, Tom decides not to invest in cryptocurrency. He knows that cryptocurrencies are highly speculative investments, and their value can be volatile. This type of investment goes against his low-risk tolerance, and he sticks with his established investment strategy.

A few months later, the cryptocurrency saw a significant drop in value, and many investors lost money. Tom's friend is among them and regrets investing in cryptocurrency. However, Tom is relieved that he decided to stick to his low-risk investment strategy. Despite missing out on the potentially high returns, he is happy with the steady and consistent returns from his bonds and blue-chip stocks.

This example demonstrates an investor's risk tolerance. By understanding his risk tolerance and sticking to his investment strategy, Tom could make a decision that aligned with his goals and helped him avoid potential losses. Tom's actions are an example of how risk tolerance can impact an investor's decision-making process.

Risk tolerance plays a crucial role in fundamental analysis investing since this can impact the types of investments an investor chooses and the mix of assets in their portfolio.

Assess the risk associated with each potential investment when conducting fundamental analysis. This includes considering factors such as the company's financial stability, the industry's competitiveness, and the potential for future growth. An investor with a high-risk tolerance may be more likely to invest in a company with high growth potential and higher financial risks. In contrast, an investor with a low-risk tolerance may prefer a more stable company with lower growth potential but lower financial risk.

Therefore, investors need to align their investment decisions with their financial goals and risk tolerance to ensure that they are comfortable with the risk level and that their investments align with their financial objectives.

The Role of Research and Due Diligence

Research and due diligence are critical components of fundamental analysis. Research is important because it allows investors to gather information about the company's financial performance, management, industry trends, and competition. By researching, investors can identify potential risks and opportunities and make informed decisions about whether to invest in a company.

Due diligence is also crucial because it helps investors verify the information they have gathered through research. This involves confirming the accuracy of the financial statements, reviewing the company's regulatory filings, and speaking with management and industry experts.

By conducting due diligence, investors can better understand a company's strengths and weaknesses, identify any red flags that could indicate problems and make informed decisions based on a comprehensive understanding of the company's financial health.

On the other hand, failing to conduct sufficient research and due diligence can lead to uninformed or poorly thought-out investment decisions, which may carry higher risks.

The Influence of Emotions and Biases

Emotions and biases can significantly impact an investor's decision-making, potentially leading to poor investment choices if not properly managed. Some common emotions and biases that can affect investment decisions include:

- **Fear and greed**: Fear of losing money or missing out on opportunities can drive investors to make impulsive decisions based on emotions rather than rational analysis. Similarly, greed can cause investors to pursue high returns at the expense of sound risk management.

- **Overconfidence**: Investors who are overconfident in their abilities may make investment decisions based on their own biases rather than considering all the available information. This can lead to over-investment in a particular stock or sector, increasing the risk of loss.
- **Anchoring bias**: This is the tendency to rely too heavily on the first piece of information encountered, even if it is not relevant or accurate. This bias can lead to irrational investment decisions based on outdated information or inaccurate assumptions.
- **Confirmation bias**: This is the tendency to seek information that confirms one's existing beliefs and ignore information that contradicts those beliefs. Confirmation bias can lead to a failure to consider alternative perspectives and result in missed investment opportunities.
- **Hindsight bias**: This is the tendency to believe that the outcome was predictable or obvious after an event has occurred. Hindsight bias can lead to overestimating one's ability to predict future events and result in irrational investment decisions.

It is important for investors to be aware of these emotions and biases and to take steps to mitigate their impact on their decision-making. This may include seeking out diverse sources of information, regularly reviewing investment decisions and outcomes, and seeking the advice of trusted advisors. Investors can make more informed and rational investment decisions by being mindful of these emotions and biases.

Another strategy is to seek diverse perspectives and viewpoints, such as consulting with a financial advisor or seeking out multiple sources of information.

Investors can also consider using mental accounting or framing tools to help make more objective and rational decisions.

Investors need to recognize that investing is inherently uncertain and should be prepared for potential gains and losses.

The Importance of Having a Diversified Portfolio

A diversified portfolio includes various assets, such as stocks, bonds, cash, and assets in different sectors and industries. Does diversification aim to spread risk across a range of assets rather than having all of an investor's eggs in one basket—recall the farmer's story in Chapter 2? Exactly!

A diversified portfolio can help investors manage risk, as it can potentially reduce the impact of any asset's performance on the overall portfolio. By diversifying, investors may also benefit from the potential growth of different types of assets rather than solely dependent on one asset's performance.

However, it is important for investors to consider the mix of assets in their portfolio carefully and to ensure that it aligns with their financial goals and risk tolerance.

For example, let's say you have been saving for your retirement for many years and have a well-diversified portfolio that includes stocks, bonds, real estate, and commodities.

One day, you hear about a major recession in the stock market. Many of your friends are selling their stock holdings, worried about losing money. However, you decide to stick to your investment strategy and not sell your stocks. You know that while the stock market may be experiencing a downturn, your other holdings in bonds, real estate, and commodities provide stability to your portfolio.

A few months later, the stock market starts to recover, and you begin to see gains in your stock holdings. Your friends, who sold their stocks during the recession, regret their decision and wish they had held on. Meanwhile, you are happy with your diversified portfolio and the fact that it helped you to manage risk during a volatile time in the stock market.

What just happened is that your diversified portfolio has helped you manage risk. By spreading your investments across different asset classes, you can reduce any one investment's impact on your portfolio's overall performance. This allowed you to weather the stock market downturn and ultimately come ahead. Diversification is an important risk management tool.

Honestly, a well-diversified portfolio can increase investors' confidence in their investment strategy, knowing that their investments are spread across a range of assets and industries. This can help investors stay the course during market volatility and maintain their focus on their long-term investment goals.

In the end, the mindset and beliefs behind fundamental analysis center around the idea that a company's long-term financial performance can be predicted by analyzing its financial statements, management quality, and economic conditions. These beliefs emphasize the importance of taking a long-term perspective, conducting thorough research, and relying on sound financial analysis when making investment decisions. By adhering to these principles, fundamental analysis can help you make informed decisions likely to result in long-term success.

However, to effectively utilize fundamental analysis, you must have skills and tools to effectively utilize fundamental analysis. Fortunately, we will discuss what these skills and tools are and how to acquire them in the next chapter.

Key Takeaways

- Having a long-term perspective can help you, as an investor, avoid being swayed by short-term market fluctuations or noise.
- Risk tolerance plays a crucial role in fundamental analysis investing since this can impact the types of investments an investor chooses and the mix of assets in their portfolio.
- Investors can make more informed and rational investment decisions by being mindful of these emotions and biases.

Chapter 5
Tools of the Trade: Essential Skills for Fundamental Analysis

> *"The stock market is filled with individuals who know the price of everything, but the value of nothing."*
> — Phillip Fisher

Anyone can buy and sell stocks. Right?

The question is, "can you do it successfully?" And that's because you can lose money.

Too often, young people simply jump into the capital market with all their money, knowing nothing, convinced they will only learn when they start trading. But the truth is that the only thing you learn when you start trading is tolerance. In essence, you need different skill sets to trade the market successfully using fundamental analysis.

Reading and interpreting financial statements, calculating financial ratios, and forecasting financial performance are all key skills required for fundamental analysis. Want to know where to start and how to develop these skills without pulling your hair out in frustration?

Well, this chapter is devoted to that task.

Of course, there are numerous paths to becoming a professional trader who has mastered the art of using fundamental analysis, but there are specific skills you need to acquire to flourish in this high-stress, highly competitive sector. For instance, when financial companies hire for trading roles, they prefer persons with degrees in math, engineering, and hard sciences over those with only finance expertise. And that shouldn't come as a surprise since these sets of people possess the unique skills needed for trading the market.

This chapter reveals these essential skills necessary for effective fundamental analysis, including how to read and interpret financial statements, calculate and interpret financial ratios, and forecast financial performance.

Research Skills:

Research skills involve gathering, evaluating, and interpreting information relevant to the stocks you pick to make informed investment decisions. They are critical for fundamental analysis in identifying investment opportunities and evaluating each investment's risks and potential rewards.

As an adept trader and investor who uses fundamental analysis, you want to be able to process standard financial data and, perhaps more importantly, have a discriminatory attitude toward financial news and information. You want to develop the ability to identify credible information relevant to the stocks you trade, and, more importantly, be able to accurately draw conclusions based on evidence.

To sharpen your research skills, you need to have a healthy thirst for information and the passion for researching all the relevant data that impacts the stocks you trade. It's important to stay up-to-date on the latest financial news and trends, read annual reports, company filings, and industry publications. You should add economic release schedules and announcements that have measurable effects on financial markets to your calendar.

You will be able to react to new information while the market is still digesting it if you stay on top of these information sources.

Analytical Thinking

Analytical thinking is an important skill for fundamental analysis, as it enables you to better understand, identify market patterns, use trends, and draw conclusions about a stock based on evidence. Analytical thinking requires attention to detail, critical thinking, and applying logic to determine what stock to trade.

Developing your analytical thinking skill will enable you to better evaluate financial statements and assess a company's financial health. It will make you focus more on taking the right action at the right time rather than just thinking about how much money you need to make from a stock. By focusing more on the market than the money in your trading account, you make the smartest, most objective trading decisions in each situation, and also make the wisest and most lucrative deals.

As a retail trader and investor, you can sharpen your analytical thinking skills by learning the basics of accounting, such as how to read and interpret financial statements, including balance sheet, income statement, and cash flow statement.

Furthermore, you want to understand financial ratios, such as the price-to-earnings ratio, return on equity, and debt-to-equity ratio, to evaluate a company's financial health and compare it to its peers in the industry.

Emotional Intelligence

If traders could simply observe the facts without emotion, they would be free of the tyranny of emotional reasoning. Then trading would be simple. But this could not be further from the truth.

The integration of emotions and reasoning in the brain makes it impossible to separate emotional feeling states from cognition and thinking. They complement each other. What is achievable, however, is the ability to govern the emotional states that give rise to a trader's cognition in a given situation. Emotional Intelligence unlocks this door.

Emotional intelligence involves the ability to manage one's emotions, understand the emotions of others, and communicate effectively. And when it comes to trading and investing in the capital market, developing your emotional intelligence enables you to become a master of the emotions that arise in stressful situations with unknown outcomes.

Acquiring emotional intelligence skills helps you to make informed investment decisions when performing fundamental analysis. It also allows you to stay calm and objective in the face of market volatility and make rational decisions based on evidence, not emotions. That way, you can manage your risks effectively.

To develop your emotional intelligence skills, you want to learn to manage your emotions, such as fear and greed, and stay focused on your investment goals. Your trading account is your most powerful ally in developing successful emotional management and beliefs.

As deceitful as emotions might be in hijacking intellect, the trading account gets right to the point. It effectively tells you how effective the beliefs you are projecting onto the markets are. It tells you which emotions and feelings shape what you see, for better or worse. It also tells you in black and white how efficient those emotional beliefs are in dealing with the unknown and uncertainty.

If your actionable beliefs are effective, you will witness an increase in the equity of your trading account. If they are ineffective, the extent of their ineffectiveness will be reflected in your Profit and Loss (P&L) Statements as drawdowns and/or stagnancy. All of this is represented in how you trade what you see and feel. You are always in a state of sensation, which shapes your view.

As a trader, you gain an advantage by mastering the emotions and mind that process information as your emotional intelligence grows. Then, feelings and information can start collaborating to form a successful trading mind. You are selecting the emotional state that will evaluate actionable market data. This is the advantage that Emotional Intelligence provides.

Psychology

Similar to emotional intelligence, psychology is another important skill required for fundamental analysis, as it involves understanding how an investor's behavior and emotions can impact investment decisions. Understanding psychology is particularly important for you as a trader/investor if you are more susceptible to emotional decision-making.

One way psychology affects fundamental analysis is through emotions like fear, greed, and overconfidence. Fear can lead to a trader making impulsive decisions, such as closing out a position too soon or not entering a trade at all, even if it has a high probability of success. On the other hand, greed can lead to taking unnecessary risks or holding onto a position for too long, hoping for an even greater return. Overconfidence can lead to ignoring warning signals, taking larger positions than usual, and being too sure of one's analysis.

Another way psychology can impact trading analysis is through biases such as confirmation bias, where you, as the investor, only look for information that confirms your pre-existing beliefs and ignore any data that contradicts them. This can lead to you taking on positions that may not align with reality or be profitable.

Although developing your psychology skills isn't easy, you can do so successfully with time. To avoid being influenced by emotions and biases when doing fundamental analysis, you should develop a trading plan that incorporates risk management strategies and considers your investment goals and risk tolerance.

You should also take a disciplined approach to trading and regularly review and evaluate your trading strategies. Finally, it's important to recognize when emotions or biases are influencing your trading decisions and take steps to address them, such as taking a break, seeking feedback from other traders, or consulting a more experienced trader.

Math and Probability

Math and probability are other important skills for fundamental analysis, as they involve the ability to analyze data and calculate risks and potential rewards. For retail investors, math and probability skills are crucial in determining the

Time-Value-Of-Money and calculating risks and potential rewards, such as estimating the potential return on investment and evaluating the risk of loss.

Developing your math and probability skills means you are learning the basics of statistics, such as how to calculate mean, median, mode, and standard deviation. It also means learning how to use tools such as Excel spreadsheets.

Spreadsheets are a tool that everyone should use, even if your only asset is a mortgaged home. When doing fundamental analysis, you will come across so many variables that can only be integrated into a model using a spreadsheet. Spreadsheets are also one of the easiest ways to keep track of the performance of your portfolio. Most crucially, other people's counsel is frequently backed up with a spreadsheet that proves their point. You must understand how to validate spreadsheets.

Sharpening your math and probability skills will also enable you to successfully make use of other financial modeling software to analyze data, make projections, and calculate the probability of different outcomes.

Creative Thinking

The capital market, in general, is changing all the time. And so, you need to be able to think outside the box to identify unique investment opportunities using fundamental analysis.

When following a rules-based strategy, the need for creative thinking is relatively low. For example, a technical trader can simply adhere to their predetermined rules for entering and exiting trades, while a passive indexer only needs to decide on the appropriate index and frequency of rebalancing.

On the other hand, a stock-picker who employs fundamental analysis must rely on their belief that the market is incorrect and that they have a better understanding of the situation. While it's true that simply being correct doesn't guarantee profits, it's possible to earn a profit when the market eventually recognizes the value of one's position.

Before delving into the market, it's important to consider whether you seek out differing viewpoints and actively search for information that may contradict your current views or whether you prefer the comfort of being surrounded by like-minded individuals.

By applying creative thinking when stock-picking, you can identify opportunities others may have overlooked and make informed investment decisions. You will also develop the willingness to challenge—a willingness to take risks and step outside the judgments that summarize past experiences.

To sharpen your creative thinking skills, it's important you explore new ideas and approaches to analyzing a stock fundamentally. This might involve reading industry publications, attending conferences or webinars, or networking with other investors or professionals. Additionally, it's important to stay curious and open-minded, and to be willing to take calculated risks in pursuit of innovative investment opportunities.

Practicing brainstorming can also help improve your creative thinking skills. This can involve picking an industry, researching a wide range of companies and their stocks in that industry, and then narrowing it down to the most promising ones. This might involve considering the impact of emerging technologies, changing consumer preferences, or regulatory trends.

Challenging your assumptions and considering multiple perspectives when evaluating investment opportunities is also important. An adept trader is one who has gained ample experience in the market. Interestingly, I've observed that most traders lack the self-assurance to forge new ideas and strategies. Instead, they rely on existing approaches that have proven successful in the past and only stumble upon new techniques when they emerge as common knowledge.

Unfortunately, by the time they recognize these innovative approaches, they may no longer be relevant or effective. As such, it's imperative for traders to embrace change and adopt a more creative and proactive approach to stay ahead in the constantly evolving market. Be open to developing and testing new concepts, as well as constantly reassessing and adjusting parameters to adapt to the ever-changing market conditions.

Basic Understanding of Economics

You also need a basic understanding of economics for fundamental analysis to enable you to understand how the economy works; how interest rates are affected and their impact; what the difference is between "a business cycle" and "an asset bubble"; what a "run on the bank" is; how inflation impacts interest yield curves, etc.

One word from the Central Bank or the President, and your asset's value can change for better or worse. The media also presents opposing economic analyses and points of view. You need to learn to read and interpret economic information to position your portfolio for the best return.

An excellent way to get started is by reading introductory economics textbooks or taking online courses in economics. This will help you understand the basic principles of microeconomics and macroeconomics, such as supply and demand, market equilibrium, and fiscal and monetary policy.

Moreover, it's also essential to stay up-to-date on economic news and trends, such as changes in interest rates, currency fluctuations, and trade policies. This will help you understand how these factors can impact investment opportunities and make informed investment decisions.

So, for example, if you're interested in investing in the technology sector, you may want to begin by researching the industry's recent performance and future growth potential. You might then consider how changes in interest rates or trade policies could impact the industry's growth potential and evaluate the risks and opportunities of investing in particular companies within the sector.

Time Management

You are probably aware of what time management is. It involves the ability to prioritize tasks, manage time effectively, and meet deadlines.

When doing fundamental analysis, time management skills are particularly important as there are various time-wasters that can suck down productivity. For example, the fundamental analysis strategy requires finding and monitoring about ten to twenty different companies, and you'll agree that it takes a lot of time and effort. It cannot be done in a spare moment or whenever you get a chance. Right?

To sharpen your time management skills, it's important to create a schedule and stick to it. Allocate specific times for market research, analysis, and decision-making. This will help you stay organized, focused, and avoid distractions. It's also important to set realistic goals and timelines for each investment decision, and break down large tasks into smaller, more manageable steps.

For example, if you're interested in investing in a particular stock, you might begin by setting a goal to research the company's financial statements and industry trends over the next few days. Once you've completed this research, you might then set a goal to evaluate the company's competitive landscape and identify potential risks and opportunities over the next few days.

Curiosity and a Continuous Desire to Learn

Everyone's career has peaks and valleys, regardless of industry, business, or specific job. If you are a full-time trader, you will surely experience huge gains and, at times, significant losses. Staying with it—remaining curious and eager to learn and develop—is an essential and necessary skill that every master trader possesses.

Of course, when favorable market fluctuations benefit your money account, it's tempting to feel enthused and overly anxious to make fast deals. Human nature compels us to continue operating in certain ways when the results are positive. But, there will be days when the market absolutely goes against you. Instead of being excited about trading, you just want to switch off your computer monitor or close up your trading platform and slink away to nurse your financial wounds.

A master trader recognizes that neither extremes will remain forever, and that having the desire to constantly learn and improve is a talent that allows you to learn, grow, and profit.

Learn to stay up-to-date on industry news and trends. Seek out new perspectives and ideas, and develop a habit of lifelong learning. This might involve taking online courses, attending seminars or workshops, or reading books and articles on a wide range of preferred industries. It's also important to seek out feedback and advice from other investors or professionals to gain new insights and perspectives on investment opportunities.

In the end, you want to make sure to master these essential skills and also that you are applying them correctly and then build on them as you develop your trading skills.

Meanwhile, even the most experienced investors can fall prey to common mistakes in fundamental analysis. The next chapter, will discuss these mistakes and how to avoid them.

Key Takeaways

- You need to have a healthy thirst for information and the passion for researching all the relevant data that impacts the stocks you trade.
- By focusing more on the market than the money in your trading account, you make the smartest, most objective trading decisions in each situation and also the wisest and most lucrative deals.
- To avoid being influenced by emotions and biases when doing fundamental analysis, you should develop a trading plan that incorporates risk management strategies and considers your investment goals and risk tolerance.
- It's also essential to stay up-to-date on economic news and trends, such as changes in interest rates, currency fluctuations, and trade policies.

Chapter 6
Avoiding the Pitfalls: Common Mistakes in Fundamental Analysis and How to Avoid Them

"In investing, what is comfortable is rarely profitable."
— *Robert Arnott*

Though fundamental analysis plays a crucial role in trading, even experienced investors make mistakes when it comes to fundamental analysis. Avoiding common pitfalls, such as relying too heavily on one source of information and ignoring the macroeconomic context, can help you make more accurate and reliable investment decisions.

Many of us have likely experienced a "blowhard" at social gatherings, boasting about their latest stock market exploits. At this particular gathering, the individual in question has taken a long position in AT&T Inc., an American multinational telecommunications holding company. You find out he knows nothing about the company he is completely in love with. He has even invested a quarter of his portfolio, hoping to quickly double his money.

However, as an informed investor, you recognize that he has fallen prey to at least four common investing mistakes, and you can't help but feel a sense of smug satisfaction. This chapter covers common mistakes that such "blowhards" make when performing fundamental analysis, and provides guidance on how to avoid these mistakes. You will also discover practical tips and strategies for avoiding these mistakes and improving the accuracy and reliability of fundamental analysis.

Mistake 1: Relying Heavily on Past Performance

One of the most common mistakes in fundamental analysis is relying too heavily on past performance. Many investors make the mistake of assuming that a company that has performed well in the past will continue to do so in the future. However, this is not always the case, as most times, they end up getting caught up in the historical success of a company or a stock. Just because a stock has performed well in the past does not mean it will continue to perform well in the future.

In 2008, investors who relied on past performance lost a significant amount of money. For example, Lehman Brothers had been a successful investment bank for over 150 years. However, the bank had a large exposure to subprime mortgages, eventually leading to its collapse in September 2008. Many investors who had relied on past performance like Lehman Brothers lost significant amounts of money as a result.

To avoid this mistake, you should focus on a company's current and future prospects, rather than past performance. You should analyze the company's current financial statements, management team, competitive landscape, and industry trends to better understand its growth potential. You should also consider any future risks or opportunities that could impact the company's performance.

For example, suppose you are considering investing in a tech company that has seen significant growth over the past few years. In that case, you want to conduct a detailed analysis of the company's financial statements to understand its current financial position, the management that leads the company, and its long-term growth potential. By focusing on the company's current and future prospects, you are sure to make more informed investment decisions.

Mistake 2: Failing to Diversify

Failing to diversify your portfolio is another terrible mistake most investors make. Diversification involves investing in a range of assets to spread risk and maximize returns. When investors fail to diversify, they risk losing their entire investment if one asset or industry underperforms.

For instance, imagine an investor who only invests in tech companies. If the tech industry experiences a downturn, the investor's portfolio will suffer significant losses. However, if the investor had diversified his portfolio by investing in different industries such as healthcare, real estate, and energy, the impact of the tech industry downturn would be less significant.

To avoid this mistake, you want to build a diverse portfolio of assets that includes different types of securities and industries. For instance, you could invest in a combination of stocks, bonds, mutual funds, and exchange-traded funds (ETFs) across various industries. Doing so reduces the risk of losses and increases your chances of achieving long-term financial goals.

Mistake 3: Not Keeping up With Changes in the Market or Industry

Another common mistake investors make is not keeping up with changes in the market or industry. The financial market is constantly changing, and new companies and trends tend to spring up every day. Failure to stay informed can lead to missed opportunities or investing in assets that are no longer viable.

For instance, let's say an investor invested in a company that produces CDs in the early 2000s. However, as technology improved, the demand for CDs decreased, and the company's revenue declined. The investor, who failed to keep up with the changes in technology and the music industry, suffered significant losses.

To avoid this mistake, investors must stay informed about market and industry trends and regularly review their investments. This can involve reading financial news, attending industry conferences, and following expert opinions on social media. Additionally, investors can set up a system for tracking and monitoring their investments, and regularly review and rebalance their portfolio to ensure that it remains aligned with their financial goals and risk tolerance.

Mistake 4: Getting Caught Up in the Hype or "Herd Mentality"

Many investors are guilty of this mistake; they get caught up in the rumors, hype, or "herd mentality." Such investors follow others' actions rather than making independent decisions based on facts and analysis. This can lead to investments that do not align with an investor's financial goals or risk tolerance.

For instance, during the cryptocurrency craze in 2017, many investors were caught up in the hype and invested heavily in cryptocurrencies without fully understanding the risks involved. Many of these investors suffered significant losses when the cryptocurrency market crashed in 2018.

To avoid this mistake, you want to conduct thorough research and analysis and make decisions based on facts, rather than being swayed by hype or the actions of others. You should also have a well-defined investment plan outlining your financial goals and risk tolerance. This plan should guide your investment decisions and help you resist the temptation to follow the herd.

Mistake 5: Being too Emotional or Biased

Investing can be an emotional experience. It is easy to get caught up in the excitement of a new investment opportunity or to become anxious or fearful when the market takes a downturn.

However, allowing emotions to drive investment decisions can lead to poor choices and missed opportunities. In fact, emotion is the number one killer of investment return. Wise investors recognize that succumbing to either of these emotions can lead to poor decision-making. Instead, it's crucial to maintain a focus on the bigger picture.

While stock market returns may fluctuate significantly in the short term, history has shown that patient investors tend to fare well over the long term. For instance, over the 10-year period leading up to May 13, 2022, the S&P 500 delivered an impressive return of 11.51%, despite the negative return of -15.57% year to date.

Investors who allow their emotions to dictate their actions may react to a negative return by panicking and selling, when holding onto their investment for the long term would have been a better choice. Furthermore, the irrational decisions of others may present opportunities for patient investors to benefit in the long run.

One of the keys to avoiding emotional decision-making is to practice emotional intelligence, which we already covered in the previous chapter. You should be aware of your own biases and emotional triggers and take steps to manage them. For example, if you find yourself getting overly excited about a new investment opportunity, take a step back and evaluate the opportunity objectively. Consider the potential risks and benefits, and research to gather all of the available information.

Mistake 6: Not Having a Clear Investment Plan or Strategy

The saying, "If you don't know where you're going, you'll likely end up somewhere else," holds as much truth in investing as it does in any other pursuit. From the overall investment plan to the specific strategies employed, the design of the portfolio, and even the choice of individual securities, every aspect of investing can be tailored to align with one's life objectives.

Investing without a clear plan or strategy is another common mistake. It can lead to haphazard decision-making and poor investment choices. Unfortunately, too many investors become fixated on the latest investment trends or the pursuit of short-term gains rather than designing an investment portfolio that has a strong likelihood of achieving their long-term objectives. By failing to focus on their ultimate goals, they risk missing out on opportunities to build a portfolio that is well-suited to their needs and priorities.

Therefore, defining your financial goals, risk tolerance, and investment strategy is important before making any investments. A clear investment plan or strategy should outline your financial objectives, the types of assets you will invest in, your investment strategy, and the level of risk you are comfortable with and stick to it. It should also include a plan for managing your investments over time, including how and when to review and rebalance your portfolio.

Mistake 7: Not Conducting Sufficient Research and Due Diligence

Many investors also fail to do enough research before making investment decisions. While some people might be tempted to rely on hot tips or rumors to guide their investing, this is a recipe for disaster. In order to make smart investment decisions, it's important to conduct thorough research and due diligence on each potential investment.

For example, suppose you're considering investing in a company that recently had a successful initial public offering (IPO). While the hype surrounding the company might be tempting, it's important to dig deeper and look at the company's financial statements, industry trends, and management team. By thoroughly researching and evaluating potential investments, including reviewing financial statements and industry trends, and seeking out multiple sources of information, you can make an informed decision about whether the investment is worth making.

Mistake 8: Chasing Short-Term Returns or Trying to Time the Market

The most basic and essential principle of investing is to purchase assets at a low price and sell them when their value is high. Despite this simple truth, why do so many investors end up doing the exact opposite? Rather than making rational and informed decisions, investment choices are often driven by the powerful forces of fear and greed.

In numerous cases, investors make the mistake of buying high in the hopes of maximizing short-term returns, instead of focusing on attaining their long-term investment objectives. This is a mistake because short-term market movements are often unpredictable, and trying to time the market is risky. Such actions are counterproductive and can hinder progress towards achieving one's financial goals.

Instead of trying to make quick profits, you want to focus on long-term goals and take a patient, disciplined approach to investing. For example, suppose you're investing in a company that you believe has strong long-term growth potential. While the stock price might fluctuate in the short term, your focus should be on the company's prospects for growth over the long term. Maintaining a long-term focus makes you less likely to make impulsive decisions based on short-term market movements.

Mistake 9: Ignoring Risks and not Having a Plan for Managing Them

Finally, it's important to consider and manage risks as part of your investment process. Investing inherently involves assuming some level of risk in exchange for the possibility of a reward. However, excessive risk-taking can lead to significant fluctuations in investment performance that may be beyond one's comfort level. Conversely, being too cautious can result in insufficient returns to meeting your financial objectives.

While there's no such thing as a risk-free investment, it's important to have a plan to manage risks and minimize potential losses. Some common strategies for managing risk include diversification, investing in low-risk assets, and having a risk management plan in place. For example, suppose you're investing in a tech company that's known for being volatile. While you believe the company has strong growth potential, you're aware of the risks associated with investing in a volatile industry. To manage these risks, you might consider diversifying your portfolio to include assets from other industries or investing in low-risk assets to balance the riskier tech investment.

It is important to be aware of your financial and emotional capacity for taking risks and understand the specific risks associated with any investment you make. By doing so, you can make informed decisions and feel more confident about your investment choices.

As with any endeavor, making mistakes is an inevitable aspect of investing. The key to success lies in recognizing these mistakes, understanding when you are making them, and taking steps to prevent their recurrence. To avoid falling into the traps discussed, it is advisable to create a well-considered and structured plan and remain committed to it. When engaging in more speculative investments, it can be helpful to designate a portion of your funds specifically for such purposes, recognizing there is a possibility of losing them.

By adhering to these principles, you can establish a solid investment portfolio that will yield significant returns over the long term and provide a sense of satisfaction and accomplishment. In addition, in order to make informed investment decisions, it is essential to have a thorough understanding of a company's industry and market position. The next chapter will explore how to evaluate these factors.

Key Takeaways

- You should focus on a company's current and future prospects rather than past performance.
- Conduct a detailed analysis of the company's financial statements to understand its current financial position, the management that leads the company, and its long-term growth potential.
- Investors must stay informed about market and industry trends and regularly review their investments. This can involve reading financial news, attending industry conferences, and following expert opinions on social media.
- While the hype surrounding the company might be tempting, it's important to dig deeper and look at its financial statements, industry trends, and management team.

Chapter 7

The Big Picture: Understanding a Company's Industry and Market Position

"Given a 10% chance of a 100 times payoff, you should take that bet every time."
— *Jeff Bezos*

Understanding a company's industry and market position is crucial for successful fundamental analysis. It is essential to have a deep understanding of the company's sector, the competitive landscape, and its market share to determine the company's potential for growth and profitability.

As the saying goes, "a rising tide lifts all boats," which means that the only real way to know if a company is worth investing in starts by studying how other industry players are performing.

You want to analyze the company's industry to determine its growth potential and the opportunities and challenges it faces. Factors such as industry trends, consumer preferences, and technological advances can significantly impact a company's performance.

Moreover, you should assess the company's market position to understand its competitive advantages and disadvantages. This includes analyzing the company's products and services, pricing strategy, and distribution channels. By understanding the company's position within its industry, you can evaluate its potential for long-term success and growth.

And that's what this chapter is all about. We will look into the importance of understanding the industry and company context in fundamental analysis, and explore the key factors to consider when evaluating an industry and company, such as competitive landscape, market trends, and business model.

Understanding a Company's Industry

Industry analysis is an evaluation technique employed by analysts and businesses to comprehend the competitive landscape of a particular industry and the firms operating in it. The aim is to gain an understanding of the industry by assessing the supply and demand statistics, the level of competition, the industry's competitiveness compared to other emerging sectors, the potential outlook for the industry considering technological advancements, the credit system within the industry, and how external factors influence it.

Understanding a company's industry is important for fundamental analysis because it informs you about the market conditions and competitive landscape in which the company operates. To research and evaluate a company's industry, you want to research and evaluate the following industry trends and factors:

- **Industry growth prospects**: Industry growth prospects refer to the potential for growth in the overall market or industry in which a company operates. One way to evaluate industry growth prospects is to look at the size of the market and its historical growth rate. It's also important to consider the factors driving growth, such as technological advancements or changes in consumer preferences. Fundamental analysts may also use market research reports and surveys to gather information about the industry's future growth prospects.

- **Trends and disruptions**: Trends and disruptions refer to changes in the market or industry that may impact a company's performance. To evaluate these factors, it's important to stay up-to-date with industry news and reports, as well as broader economic trends that may affect the market. Fundamental analysts may also use data analytics tools to identify emerging trends, such as changes in consumer behavior or shifts in demand for certain products or services.

- **Competitive landscape**: The competitive landscape refers to the other companies operating in the same industry as the company being analyzed. To evaluate the competitive landscape, it's important to research the strengths and weaknesses of each competitor, as well as their market share and financial performance. You also want to look at pricing strategies, marketing campaigns, and other factors that may impact a company's ability to compete in the market.

- **Regulatory environment**: The regulatory environment refers to the laws and regulations that affect the industry in which a company operates. To evaluate the regulatory environment, it's important to research the relevant laws and regulations and any proposed changes that may impact the industry. You should also look at the company's compliance history and any pending legal or regulatory issues that may affect its performance.

- **Supply chain dynamics**: Supply chain dynamics refers to the flow of goods and services from the suppliers to the company and from the company to its customers. To evaluate supply chain dynamics, it's important to understand the suppliers and customers of the company being analyzed and any intermediaries in the supply chain. You may also evaluate the cost and efficiency of the supply chain, as well as any potential risks or disruptions that may impact the company's operations.

By understanding a company's industry, you can better assess the potential risks and opportunities that may impact the company's performance.

Industry Trends and Competitive Analysis

Earlier, we talked about researching and evaluating trends and disruptions and the competitive landscape as part of understanding a company's industry for fundamental analysis.

We talked about how understanding industry trends and the competitive landscape can help investors better understand a company's position within its market and the challenges and opportunities it may face. Right?

But there's more…

Identifying and analyzing key industry trends and competitors also involves conducting research, reviewing financial statements, and considering factors such as market share, product offerings, and competitive strategies.

Before we go on to discuss how to identify and analyze key industry trends and competitors, I want to briefly explain the importance of understanding industry trends and the competitive landscape in fundamental analysis.

By doing so, you can evaluate a company's financial performance and growth potential in its industry. Industry trends can significantly impact a company's revenue, earnings, and growth prospects. For example, emerging technologies or changes in consumer preferences can create new opportunities for growth, while increased competition or regulatory changes can present significant challenges for established companies.

By analyzing the competitive landscape, you can evaluate a company's position in its industry relative to its peers. This includes assessing the company's market share, pricing power, and ability to innovate and adapt to changing market conditions. Understanding a company's competitive position can provide valuable insights into its growth potential and long-term sustainability.

Now that we are on the same page, let's go on to discuss how to identify and analyze key industry trends and competitors.

- **Focus on industries with favorable long-term growth prospects**: You want to focus on those with favorable long-term growth prospects. For example, over the past decade or so, the percentage of retail sales that take place online has grown from less than 5% to more than 11% today. So e-commerce is an example of an industry with a favorable growth trend. Cloud computing, payments technology, and healthcare are a few other industries that will likely grow significantly in the years ahead.

- **Conduct research**: The first step is to research the industry in which the company operates. Look for industry reports, news articles, and publications that discuss the trends, opportunities, and challenges in the industry. This will help you get a broad understanding of the industry and identify the key drivers of growth and profitability.

- **Review financial statements**: Next, review the company's financial statements, such as its income statement, balance sheet, and cash flow statement. Look for trends in revenue growth, profit margins, and cash flow that indicate the company's financial health and performance over time. Compare the company's financial performance to other companies in the industry to get a sense of its competitive position.

- **Consider competitive factors**: Finally, consider the competitive landscape in which the company operates. Look at factors such as market share, product offerings, pricing strategies, and competitive advantages. Identify the company's competitors and analyze their strengths and weaknesses. This will help you understand the company's competitive position and potential growth opportunities. (More on this subject in the fourth section of this chapter).

Finally, you want to always stay up-to-date on industry developments as it can help you to stay informed about emerging trends and changes in the market. This includes keeping track of news, regulations, and emerging technologies that may impact the industry in the short and long term.

Investors can stay up-to-date by regularly reading industry publications, attending conferences and trade shows, monitoring social media and online forums, and following industry experts and analysts. You can also conduct surveys and interviews with industry stakeholders to better understand the market dynamics and trends.

By staying informed, you can make more informed investment decisions based on the current and expected conditions of the industry, including any potential opportunities or risks.

Market Conditions and Macroeconomic Factors

Companies tend to experience growth during economic upswings more than during downturns. When businesses and consumers feel the economy is strong, they tend to spend more money, creating more demand for goods and services. Companies can respond by increasing production, hiring more workers, and building inventory to meet the rising demand, fueling the growth cycle.

However, when there is uncertainty about the economy's future, businesses and individuals tend to save rather than spend, causing higher unemployment and less production. Companies may find they have overestimated their production needs and must cut back during an economic slowdown, slowing overall economic growth even further.

To understand market conditions and macroeconomic factors, you want to pay attention to the following:

- **Economic growth**: When the economy looks poor, investors may sell down equity positions or be more selective about which positions they take on, while a strong economy gives investors confidence in the equity market. To a large extent, economic growth is driven by two major factors: consumer spending and business investment. The Gross Domestic Product (GDP) is a common measure of economic growth and represents the total value of goods and services produced by a country over the course of a year.

- **Unemployment**: High unemployment restricts consumer spending, with consumers allocating their funds only to essential items, affecting companies' earning capacity and stock prices. Consumer staples and defensive sectors tend to perform better in high unemployment environments. Rather than just looking at the monthly figures, analysts tend to focus on the trend in the unemployment rate, which is used to gauge inflationary and interest rate expectations. Inflation is likely to increase when the unemployment rate falls below the Non-Accelerating Inflation Rate of Unemployment (NAIRU) level.

- **Inflation:** Rising costs impact businesses' profits, with input prices being higher. This may restrict consumers' spending on non-essential items, affecting business earnings and stock prices. High inflation can be a signal that the economy is overheating, while moderate inflation can be associated with economic growth as it indicates that businesses and consumers are spending more money on goods and services. Traders also keep an eye on the Consumer Price Index (CPI) and Producer Price Index (PPI) as well as other inflationary pressures.

- **Interest rates**: High interest rates can impede business growth by restricting borrowing capacity, affecting earnings growth and stock prices. Consumers may also experience increased mortgage interest payments, reducing their purchasing power, and causing less demand for non-essential goods and services, affecting company earnings and stock prices. Stocks tend to sell off when there is talk of a rate hike in the future.

Overall, if interest rates rise, consumer spending and investment tends to decrease, which can result in lower economic growth and inflation. Central banks often use interest rates to manage inflation and support economic growth.

Understanding and considering these factors can help you, as an investor, to better assess the risks and opportunities associated with an investment. Tools such as economic indicators and financial news sources can help stay informed about market conditions and macroeconomic factors.

Analyzing a Company's Competitive Advantage

A competitive advantage is a unique attribute or capability that allows a company to offer a superior product or service and differentiate itself from competitors. Competitive advantage refers to a company's ability to outperform its rivals in producing goods and/or services, either by offering better quality or lower costs. For instance, a business may excel in customer service or benefit from economies of scale, allowing it to produce products more affordably. Possessing one or more competitive advantages places a company in an advantageous position to successfully implement its business strategy and expand sustainably compared to its competitors.

A company's competitive advantage can also be identified as its "unique selling proposition," which is the exceptional reason that entices customers to repeatedly purchase a company's products or services. Perhaps you appreciate a product's low price. Maybe you like the product because it's unique in the marketplace and no other company produces anything with the same functionality. Or, perhaps, you simply value the customer service provided by the company.

Evaluating a company's competitive advantage is important for fundamental analysis because it helps investors understand its **unique value proposition** and how it can sustain its competitive edge over time.

To identify a company's competitive advantage, you want to consider the following factors:

- **Product or service offerings**: A company can have a competitive advantage if it offers a unique product or service that cannot be easily replicated by competitors. To evaluate a company's product or service offerings, you can look at factors such as product differentiation, innovation, and quality. A company that can offer products or services of higher quality or more innovative than its competitors can gain a competitive advantage.

- **Pricing strategy**: A company can also have a competitive advantage based on its pricing strategy. A company that can offer lower prices than its competitors while still maintaining profitability can attract more customers and gain market share. On the other hand, a company that can charge higher prices for its products or services based on factors such as superior quality or brand reputation can also have a competitive advantage.

- **Brand reputation**: A company's brand reputation can also be a key factor in its competitive advantage. A strong brand reputation can help a company attract and retain customers and can also provide a level of protection against competition. To evaluate a company's brand reputation, you can look at factors such as brand recognition, customer loyalty, and customer satisfaction ratings.

- **Distribution channels**: A company's distribution channels can also play a role in its competitive advantage. A company with an efficient and effective distribution network can reach more customers and deliver products or services faster and more reliably than its competitors. To evaluate a company's distribution channels, you can look at factors such as the number of distribution channels, the efficiency of the distribution network, and the ability to adapt to changes in customer demand.

- **Patent or intellectual property protection**: A company with strong patent or intellectual property protection can also have a competitive advantage. A company that has patents or proprietary technology that competitors cannot easily replicate can maintain a dominant market position. To evaluate a company's patent or intellectual property protection, you can look at factors such as the number of patents, the strength of the patents, and the ability to defend against infringement.

- **Sustainability**: A company with a strong commitment to sustainability can also have a competitive advantage. Consumers are increasingly seeking out products and services that are environmentally friendly and socially responsible. To evaluate a company's sustainability practices, you can look at factors such as the use of renewable resources, waste reduction initiatives, social responsibility programs, and the company's ability to adapt to changing market conditions.

Apple (NASDAQ: AAPL) is a good example of a company with several competitive advantages over other companies in the tech industry. Firstly, the company is known for its visually appealing, minimalist-inspired products that outperform its competitors. Mac devices, in particular, are less prone to the bugs and issues that are commonly associated with Windows computers, giving Apple a significant edge in terms of product quality. Additionally, Apple has made it easy for customers to integrate its devices across multiple product lines, which further cements the company's competitive advantage.

Another factor contributing to Apple's competitive advantage is the customer experience it provides. The company has made the buying process simple and seamless, whether customers choose to make purchases online or in-store. In-store paperwork is completed on tablets, and purchases can be made via computers, smartphones, or watches. By making it easy to be a customer, Apple has been able to create significant brand loyalty, which is a key factor in the company's success. This loyalty allows Apple to continue releasing new versions of the same product and still grow its revenues.

Assessing Industry and Market Risks

Risk assessment is a broad word that refers to determining the likelihood of loss on an asset, loan, or investment. Risk assessment is critical to establishing the worthiness of a certain investment and the best process(es) to manage risk. It displays the potential benefit in relation to the risk profile. Risk assessment is necessary to calculate the rate of return required by an investor to consider an investment worth the potential risk.

Assessing industry and market risks is important for fundamental analysis because it helps investors understand the potential risks that may impact a company's performance.

To assess industry and market risks, investors can consider the following factors:

- **Regulatory changes**: These can have a significant impact on companies and industries. To assess regulatory risks, investors should keep up-to-date with changes to regulations that affect their investments. For example, a new environmental regulation could impact companies in the energy sector, leading to increased costs or fines for non-compliance.

- **Competitive landscape**: An industry's competitive landscape can also significantly impact individual companies. Investors should evaluate the competitive environment to understand how it could affect a company's performance. For example, a new entrant with disruptive technology could significantly impact the market share of existing players.
- **Market trends**: Market trends are an important consideration when assessing industry and market risks. Trends such as changing consumer preferences, demographic shifts, or technological advances can significantly impact industries and companies. Investors should consider the potential impacts of these trends on a company's products, services, and operations.
- **Economic conditions**: Economic conditions, such as interest rates, inflation, and unemployment rates, can have a significant impact on industries and companies. For example, a recession could lead to decreased demand for luxury goods, impacting retail or fashion industry companies.
- **Technological disruptions**: Technological disruptions are another important consideration when assessing industry and market risks. For example, the rise of e-commerce has disrupted traditional retail businesses. Investors should consider the potential impact of new technologies on the companies they are evaluating.

By identifying and evaluating potential risks, you will be in a better position to understand the potential impact on a company and make more informed investment decisions. It is also important for investors to consider how a company is positioning itself to manage and mitigate these risks.

Next up in our qualitative analysis is evaluating a company's management team. A company's leadership can have a major impact on its success or failure, so it's important to carefully consider this factor as you make investment decisions.

Key Takeaways

- Understanding a company's industry is important for fundamental analysis because it informs you about the market conditions and competitive landscape in which the company operates.

- Identifying and analyzing key industry trends and competitors involves conducting research, reviewing financial statements, and considering factors such as market share, product offerings, and competitive strategies.

- Assessing industry and market risks is important for fundamental analysis because it helps investors to understand the potential risks that may impact a company's performance.

Chapter 8
The Boss Squad: Evaluating a Company's Management Team

"We don't prognosticate macroeconomic factors; we're looking at our companies from a bottom-up perspective on their long-run prospects of returning."
— Mellody Hobson

Warren Buffett famously said, "I try to buy stock in businesses that are so wonderful that an idiot can run them, because sooner or later, one will."

That's right! In fact, I couldn't agree more.

Once a leading innovator in the personal computing industry, Apple's performance had dwindled in the 1990s. By the mid-90s, Apple was in dire straits, with declining sales and a lack of direction. The company struggled to keep pace with competitors such as Microsoft, and many analysts predicted that Apple would soon be out of business.

In 1997, Apple's board of directors made a bold move by bringing back Steve Jobs, one of the company's co-founders, as its CEO. Jobs, who had been ousted from the company in the mid-1980s, quickly set about turning Apple's fortunes around.

Jobs understood that Apple needed a fresh start and a new direction. He immediately implemented several key changes, including streamlining Apple's product line, cutting costs, and investing in research and development to produce innovative new products.

Jobs was also a master marketer, and he understood the importance of creating a strong brand identity. He oversaw the development of Apple's iconic "Think Different" ad campaign, which helped reinvigorate the company's image and generate buzz around its products.

One of Jobs' most significant contributions to Apple was the introduction of the iMac, a revolutionary all-in-one personal computer widely regarded as a game-changer in the industry. Jobs followed up the success of the iMac with other groundbreaking products, including the iPod, iPhone, and iPad.

Under Jobs' leadership, Apple transformed from a struggling company on the brink of collapse into one of the most successful and influential technology companies in the world. Jobs' vision and leadership helped Apple revolutionize the personal computing, music, and mobile phone industries, and cemented his legacy as one of the greatest innovators of his time.

So, you would agree that the management team of a company has a huge role to play in terms of growth. And that's why we want to find out how to evaluate a company's management and leadership in this chapter. We will examine the role of management and leadership in the success of a company. This chapter also covers the key factors to consider when evaluating the management team, such as experience, track record, and leadership style.

The Role of Management in a Company's Success

Business owners often hold the misconception that their personal involvement in managing all aspects of their operations directly determines the value of their business.

However, this is not the case. What is transferable to the buyer is the attractiveness of the business, not the ongoing management skills of the seller. If the owner relies heavily on personal involvement and has a management team that cannot sustain the business's growth without the owner, then the business represents little value to a buyer and has significant future risk. Although this may seem counterintuitive to some owners, the fact remains that if a business cannot survive and grow without the owner's daily interaction, its value will dramatically diminish regardless of past growth and profits.

According to Peter Drucker, a top management consultant, creating a successful enterprise requires building a top management team well in advance of when it is needed and well before it can be afforded.

Most professional buyers, including private equity groups, evaluate the value of the companies they consider acquiring by assessing the strength of the company's value drivers, with management being the most important. These investors recognize the value of great management teams and often prefer to acquire a company with strong management already in place, rather than bringing in outside managers.

Thus, a company's management team is crucial to its success or failure. The management is responsible for making key decisions that impact the direction of the company and its performance. These include setting strategic goals and objectives, making financial and operational plans, and leading and motivating employees.

A strong management team can contribute to a company's growth and stability, while a weak or ineffective team can hinder a company's performance. Here are the various responsibilities and tasks of a management team:

- **Decision-making**: The management team is responsible for making strategic decisions that guide the direction of the company. This includes decisions related to new product development, investments, mergers and acquisitions, and other important business activities.
- **Strategy**: The management team is also responsible for developing and implementing the company's overall strategy. This includes identifying new growth opportunities, analyzing market trends, and developing plans to achieve long-term goals.
- **Leadership**: The management team sets the tone for the company's culture and values. They are responsible for leading by example and creating a positive work environment that fosters collaboration, creativity, and innovation.
- **Financial management**: The management team is responsible for managing the company's financial resources. This includes budgeting, financial planning, and ensuring that the company is operating in a financially sustainable manner. They are also responsible for managing relationships with investors and lenders.

Overall, the management team is critical to the success of a company. As an investor, it is important to evaluate the management team's track record, their ability to make sound decisions, and their ability to execute their plans. Doing so lets you gain insight into the company's long-term potential and make more informed investment decisions.

How to Evaluate a Company's Management Team

Having realized how much it is for a company to have a good management team, the problem would be evaluating management. There are many intangible aspects of a job, and investors cannot solely rely on financial statements to understand a company. Examples like Enron, Worldcom, and Imclone have highlighted the significance of focusing on the qualitative aspects of a company.

While some argue that qualitative factors are irrelevant, as a company's financial performance and stock price are indicative of the value of management, this perspective does not necessarily hold true. While strong performance over a longer period may reflect good management, this is not always the case in the short term. A prime example is the rise and fall of dotcoms, which at one point was lauded as a new generation of business leaders who would revolutionize the industry, with their high stock prices being taken as a sign of success. However, the market's unpredictable nature means that a robust stock performance alone is not an accurate reflection of the quality of management.

Thus, it's important we pay detailed attention to this subject when doing fundamental analysis. The following are the various factors and considerations to take into account when evaluating management as part of the fundamental analysis process:

- **Length of tenure**: The duration that a CEO and top management serve a company can be an effective gauge of performance. A prime example is General Electric, where former CEO Jack Welch led for approximately two decades and earned a reputation as one of the most successful managers ever. Warren Buffett also values management retention highly at Berkshire Hathaway, where he looks for stable, reliable leadership when evaluating potential investments.

- **Corporate strategy and goals**: It's essential to examine the objectives that the management has set out for the company. A well-defined mission statement can offer clear direction for employees, shareholders, and partners, while a vague statement packed with jargon raises red flags. Ideally, a robust mission statement should outline attainable and measurable goals that align with the company's long-term vision.

- **Insider buying and stock buybacks**: When insiders buy shares in their company, it can suggest that they possess non-public information, which could be a positive indicator. Regular insider buying indicates that management is committed to the business, but it's equally important to scrutinize the duration that the management holds the shares. Similarly, stock buybacks can be an effective use of company resources when the business is undervalued and returns shareholder value.

- **Compensation**: Compensation for high-level executives is generally justified, as strong leadership can significantly enhance shareholder value. However, it can be challenging to determine what level of compensation is reasonable. Industry disparities exist, with CEOs in the banking sector earning substantially more than their counterparts in retail or food service. Therefore, it's advisable to compare CEO pay within the same industry, and it's bothersome if an executive earns an excessively high salary while the company performs poorly.

- **Management communication**: When investing in a stock for the long-term, you need a management team that is very communicative, which means relaying any problems to investors upfront when it occurs and not months or years later when the problem may already be affecting the business model and stock price. The ways a management team would use to communicate include shareholder letters, management discussion and analysis, (MD&A), company announcements, mission statement, and company policy.

As an investor, you can also assess the management team's alignment with shareholder interests, their ability to adapt to changes in the market or industry, and their overall vision for the company. By carefully evaluating a company's management team, you can gain insight into the company's potential for success and make more informed investment decisions.

Common Mistakes When Evaluating Management

Want to avoid the next Enron, Worldcom, or Valeant?

Then you may want to pay more attention to this section. CEOs such as Warren Buffett, Mark Leonard, Jeff Bezos, and Satya Nadella are prime examples of how effective management can greatly influence a company's success.

The management team plays a crucial role in guiding a company, and choosing the wrong leader poses a significant risk. At times, even the founder may not be the ideal leader, as they may excel at creating great products but struggle as a leader, while in other cases, they may turn out to be excellent leaders.

Below are strategies to avoiding these mistakes and improving the accuracy of your assessment. As an investor, you want to avoid these common mistakes when evaluating a company's management team.

- **Failing to consider the management team's track record or past performance**: A company's performance is highly dependent on the quality of its management team. However, investors often overlook the track record and past performance of the team. Reviewing the management team's history to evaluate their ability to lead a company and achieve its objectives is essential.

- **Overlooking potential red flags or warning signs**: Investors, sometimes, overlook potential warning signs when assessing a management team's quality. For example, a history of conflicts or legal issues could be a red flag that needs further investigation. It's crucial to look beyond the surface level and dig deeper to uncover any potential issues.

- **Not asking enough questions or seeking out enough information**: Investors must ask the right questions and seek out enough information to make an informed decision. Investors should inquire about their experience, track record, and management style when evaluating the management team. Additionally, investors can look at industry publications, analyst reports, and financial news to gain insight into the company's management.

- **Being swayed by charisma or superficial qualities rather than substance**: Investors can be swayed by a management team's charisma or outward appearances rather than focusing on their substance. While charisma is important, investors should not overlook the team's management style, industry experience, and decision-making processes. It's critical to look beyond the surface and evaluate the team's leadership qualities and financial management skills.

To avoid these mistakes, you want to take a more thorough and critical approach to evaluating management, including reviewing the team's experience and track record, asking questions, and seeking out multiple sources of information.

The next chapter will discuss why a corporation's sense of ethics is an important factor to consider in fundamental analysis.

Key Takeaways

- A company's management team plays a crucial role in its success or failure.
- A strong management team can contribute to a company's growth and stability, while a weak or ineffective team can hinder a company's performance.
- It's essential to review the management team's history to evaluate their ability to lead a company and achieve its objectives.

Chapter 9

Corporate Governance: Making Sure a Company is run Ethically and Responsibly

"The individual investor should act consistently as an investor and not as a speculator."
— Ben Graham

Corporate governance ensures that a company is run ethically and responsibly. But what exactly does that involve, and why is it so important for investors?

Let's say there's a company with a board of directors made up of the CEO's friends and family. The board is known for rubber-stamping the CEO's decisions without much questioning, and the company is performing poorly as a result.

One day, an activist investor takes notice and decides to take action. The investor then starts a campaign to replace the current board members with independent directors who have relevant experience and a track record of holding management accountable.

The campaign gains support from other shareholders, who are tired of the company's underperformance and lack of accountability. Eventually, the board is replaced with a new, independent group of directors who brings fresh ideas and a renewed focus on corporate governance.

Under the new board's leadership, the company implements new policies and practices that improve transparency, accountability, and performance. The company's share price and financial performance begins to improve, and the company regains the trust and confidence of its investors and stakeholders.

This illustration here highlights the importance of corporate governance and the role of independent directors in ensuring a company's long-term success. As a trader or investor, you want to pay attention to a company that only has a board of directors composed of qualified, independent members willing to ask tough questions, hold management accountable, and act in the best interests of the company and its stakeholders.

So let's explore what corporate governance is, its importance in fundamental analysis, and key factors to consider when evaluating a company's corporate governance practices.

What is Corporate Governance?

Corporate governance is the set of rules, procedures, and processes that guide and control a firm. It entails balancing the interests of a company's numerous stakeholders, which include shareholders, management, consumers, suppliers, financiers, the government, and the community.

By adhering to principles of transparency and accountability, good corporate governance can safeguard against corporate scandals, fraud, and potential issues related to corporate liability. An organization that is structured and culturally aligned with such principles can prevent major calamities like the collapse of Enron.

As an investor, it's important you check how good the corporate governance of a company is before buying its stock. Doing so helps ensure that a company is being run ethically and responsibly, which can positively impact the company's performance and value.

Boards of directors play a key role in corporate governance, as they are responsible for overseeing the management of a company and making strategic decisions. Other key players in corporate governance include shareholders, who have the right to vote on certain matters affecting the company, and executive management, who are responsible for the day-to-day running of the company.

Boards must be ready to address a multitude of inquiries from shareholders. Shareholders expect the chairman of the board to be distinct from the CEO. They may also request information about the number of boards on which each board director serves to ensure they have enough time to fulfill their duties. It is typical for shareholders to expect that most, if not all, board directors are independent.

Shareholders may also raise questions about each board director's ownership stake in the company and whether there are any conflicts of interest or personal relationships between the board and management. Shareholders may seek information about management's pay structure and disclosure, as well as the board's remuneration. Shareholders may want assurance that the board has not approved excessively generous stock options that could harm their investment in the future.

Simple, a robust system of corporate governance is recognized and valued by shareholders, stakeholders, employees, and customers, and can significantly impact a company's reputation. The effectiveness of a company's corporate governance practices can either increase or decrease its valuation.

Corporate Governance Principles and Frameworks

There are various principles and frameworks that guide corporate governance practices. These principles and frameworks outline the expectations and standards for good corporate governance, including issues such as transparency, accountability, fairness, and responsibility.

Equitable treatment of shareholders, regardless of their level of ownership, is a fundamental principle of corporate governance. Each shareholder has the right to a voice at the annual general meeting, and the board of directors must align with shareholders on the company's mission, vision, values, and culture.

In addition to establishing a code of conduct, boards must also ensure that they avoid conflicts of interest and demonstrate ethical behavior and integrity. Board members should exemplify the company's values as part of the corporate culture. Strong governance ensures that companies remain compliant and out of trouble.

To practice good governance, boards must consider the interests and concerns of all stakeholders. Establishing a trustworthy relationship with stakeholders enhances the company's reputation, improves its relationship with the community, and allows it to handle media requests responsibly and accurately.

The transparency of financial records and earnings reports is of utmost importance. All financial documents should be easily accessible, accurately stated, and transparent for review.

Adhering to these principles and frameworks can help to promote ethical and responsible behavior within a company, and can improve the company's reputation and performance.

It is important for investors to be aware of these principles and frameworks and to consider how a company's corporate governance practices align with them when making investment decisions.

Evaluating a Company's Corporate Governance Practices

Investors can evaluate a company's corporate governance practices by reviewing the company's corporate governance policies and reports and by gathering information from other sources such as news articles, ratings agencies, and shareholder advocacy groups.

Now, let's look at the types of information and resources that investors can use to evaluate a company's corporate governance, focusing on six key areas.

1. **Board composition, independence, and effectiveness**

When evaluating a company's corporate governance, investors should pay close attention to the composition of the board, the independence of its members, and its overall effectiveness. A diverse board, with a mix of expertise and experience, can help bring different perspectives and promote more effective decision-making. Independent directors, who are not employees of the company, are also important as they can better act in the interests of shareholders rather than management.

One important resource for investors looking to evaluate a company's board is the proxy statement—a document companies must file with the SEC before their annual shareholder meeting. The proxy statement provides detailed information about the company's board, including the names and biographical information of the directors, the number of shares they own, and their compensation.

2. **Executive compensation and management practices**

Executive compensation is another critical aspect of corporate governance, and investors should be wary of companies that offer excessive or unjustified compensation to their top executives. Investors can evaluate executive compensation by reviewing the company's proxy statement and examining the salaries, bonuses, and other benefits provided to top executives. You should also evaluate the company's management practices, such as its succession plan and talent development programs, to ensure that it has a strong pipeline of talent to lead the company into the future.

3. **Shareholder rights and engagement**

Shareholder rights and engagement are critical to ensuring that companies are held accountable to their shareholders. Investors should evaluate a company's corporate governance by looking at its policies regarding shareholder rights, including the ability to vote on key issues and nominate directors to the board. You should also consider the company's track record in engaging with shareholders and addressing their concerns, such as through regular shareholder meetings and responsiveness to shareholder proposals.

4. **Transparency and disclosure**

Transparency and disclosure are critical to ensuring that companies operate responsibly and ethically, and investors should evaluate a company's corporate governance by examining its policies and practices in these areas. This includes evaluating the company's financial reporting and accounting practices and its social and environmental responsibility policies. Investors should also evaluate the company's history of disclosing information to its shareholders and the public and its responsiveness to requests for information.

5. **Governance ratings or rankings**

There are several organizations that provide ratings or rankings of companies based on their corporate governance practices. These ratings can be a useful resource for investors looking to evaluate a company's governance, as they provide an objective and standardized assessment of a company's practices. Examples of such organizations include MSCI, which produces a corporate governance index that ranks companies based on their governance practices, and Institutional Shareholder Services (ISS), which provides a range of ratings and analyses of corporate governance practices.

6. **Corporate governance practices**

Finally, it is important for investors to consider a company's corporate governance practices as part of their overall investment decision-making process, as good corporate governance can be an indicator of a company's overall health and stability.

Investors can evaluate a company's corporate governance practices by examining its overall approach to governance. This includes examining its policies and procedures related to risk management, internal controls, and compliance with laws and regulations.

Along with ethics and values, incorporating social and environmental responsibility into your investment decisions is a personal choice, but it can have a major impact on both the companies you invest in and the world at large. The next chapter will explore the role of these factors in fundamental analysis.

Key Takeaways

- Corporate governance involves balancing the interests of a company's numerous stakeholders, which includes shareholders, management, consumers, suppliers, financiers, the government, and the community.
- To practice good governance, boards must consider the interests and concerns of all stakeholders.
- Investors can evaluate a company's corporate governance practices by reviewing the company's corporate governance policies and reports and by gathering information from various sources.

Chapter 10

Doing Good While Doing Well: The Importance of Social and Environmental Responsibility in Investing

"I don't look to jump over seven-foot bars; I look around for one-foot bars that I can step over."
— *Warren Buffett*

While corporate governance is a good starting point for evaluating a company's ethical values, it's also worth assessing their social and environmental footprints.

As reports of unethical and illicit investment practices become more frequent, many investors now require the companies they invest in to prioritize social and environmental responsibility.

These responsible companies are expected to operate in an environmentally conscious manner, provide their employees with good working conditions, produce healthy products and services, and avoid unethical or exploitative business practices. For both these companies and their stakeholders, investing is not simply a matter of generating profits and increasing wealth but also cultivating a sustainable and socially responsible enterprise.

This chapter covers the role of social and environmental responsibility in fundamental analysis. We will discuss the importance of considering a company's impact on stakeholders and the environment, and cover the key factors to consider when evaluating a company's social and environmental practices.

The Role of Social and Environmental Responsibility in Investing

Social and environmental responsibility has become an increasingly important consideration for investors, as more people are looking to align their investments with their values. This practice is what some investors refer to as *responsible investing*.

Responsible investing, also known as socially responsible investing, involves investing money in companies and funds that positively impact society. By seeking out funds with companies that align with your values, you can support businesses that engage in social justice, environmental sustainability, clean energy, diversity initiatives, or women's leadership. Conversely, you can avoid supporting companies that engage in non-environmental practices like coal-mining or addictions such as alcohol, tobacco, or gambling.

Investing with social and environmental responsibility is important because it provides the opportunity to generate returns while contributing to causes that matter to you. Remember, socially responsible investments are still investments, so it's essential to consider their risks, benefits, and potential returns to ensure that your money generates good returns while also aligning with your social goals.

For instance, investing in socially and environmentally responsible companies can positively impact society and the environment and may also be a source of long-term financial returns. On the other hand, investing in companies that are not socially and environmentally responsible may carry risks, such as reputational damage or regulatory challenges.

Let's just quickly discuss the other benefits and risks in detail, and also, how they can impact the value of a company.

- **Enhances long-term investment performance**: Socially and environmentally responsible companies may be better positioned to generate higher returns over the long term because they are more likely to have sustainable business practices that promote growth and stability.
- **Positive impact**: By investing in socially and environmentally responsible companies, investors can support businesses that have a positive impact on society and the environment. For example, these companies may have initiatives to reduce their carbon footprint, protect natural resources, or promote social justice.
- **Risk management**: Companies with strong social and environmental practices may be better positioned to manage risks and avoid legal, repu-

tational, and financial issues arising from negative social or environmental impacts.

- **Attract and retain talent**: Companies prioritizing social and environmental responsibility are more likely to attract and retain talented employees who value these principles. This can lead to a more motivated and engaged workforce, which can ultimately translate into better business performance.

Risks of investing in socially and environmentally responsible companies:

- **Limited investment opportunities**: Socially and environmentally responsible investing is a relatively new field, and there may be fewer investment opportunities available, particularly in certain sectors or regions.
- **Lower returns**: Investing in socially and environmentally responsible companies may come at a cost, as companies with these practices may be less profitable in the short term. Investors should be prepared to accept lower returns in exchange for the positive impact they seek.
- **Limited track record**: Because socially and environmentally responsible investing is a relatively new field, there may be limited data available to assess the performance of these investments over the long term. As a result, it may be challenging to evaluate the potential risks and returns associated with these investments.
- **Subjectivity and lack of standardization**: The standards and criteria for socially and environmentally responsible investing may be subjective and vary across different investors and investment managers. There is a lack of standardization and consistency in measuring the impact and performance of these investments.
- **Market volatility**: Socially and environmentally responsible companies may be exposed to risks unique to their business practices, such as regulatory changes, shifts in consumer preferences, or reputational issues. These risks can lead to market volatility, which can impact the returns of the investment.

While it's hard to attach a hard number to the financial impact that a company's social and environmental footprint can have on a company's short-term stock performance, these factors can shed light on its long-term value.

How to Assess a Company's Social and Environmental Impact

The task of measuring a company's impact on social and environmental issues is a crucial and intricate undertaking that extends beyond merely reporting metrics. It encompasses various aspects, such as mitigating harm or benefiting stakeholders, as well as contributing to solutions for social and environmental problems.

Measuring a company's social and environmental impact is crucial in evaluating the attainment of sustainable objectives, but it is still not fully comprehended by many, who may not know how to measure their impact or manage it effectively. The following tools and resources are what you can use, as an investor, to assess a company's social and environmental impact.

Sustainability reports

A sustainability report is a document that provides a comprehensive overview of a company's economic, social, and environmental performance. These reports provide detailed information on a company's sustainability practices, such as energy efficiency, waste reduction, water conservation, employee health and safety, and community involvement.

When analyzing a sustainability report, you should look for information on a company's environmental and social impact, governance practices, and stakeholder engagement. You should also consider the company's goals, initiatives, and progress toward achieving sustainability objectives.

Rating agencies

These are independent organizations that evaluate companies based on their environmental, social, and governance (ESG) performance. These agencies provide a score or rating that reflects a company's commitment to sustainable practices.

Some of the most well-known ratings agencies include MSCI ESG, Sustainalytics, and the Carbon Disclosure Project (CDP). These agencies use a range of criteria to assess a company's ESG performance, including its carbon footprint, energy efficiency, labor practices, supply chain management, and transparency.

You can use ratings agencies to assess a company's sustainability practices and compare them to industry peers. Ratings agencies may also provide a detailed breakdown of a company's ESG score, highlighting areas of strength and weakness. However, it's important to note that ratings agencies may have different methodologies and criteria, so investors should consider multiple sources before making an investment decision.

Specialized indexes

Specialized indexes are investment benchmarks focusing on companies with strong ESG performance. These indexes are designed to track the performance of companies that meet specific sustainability criteria.

Some of the most well-known specialized indexes include the Dow Jones Sustainability Index, the FTSE4Good Index, and the MSCI World ESG Leaders Index. These indexes use a range of criteria to assess a company's ESG performance, such as carbon emissions, energy efficiency, labor practices, and governance.

You can use specialized indexes to invest in companies with a strong commitment to sustainable practices. Investing in a specialized index can provide diversification and potentially generate a competitive return, while also supporting companies with positive social and environmental impact.

Investors can also look for information on a company's supply chain, employee practices, and community engagement to understand its overall social and environmental performance.

Meanwhile, it is important for investors to be thorough and consider multiple sources of information when evaluating a company's social and environmental impact.

Investing in Socially and Environmentally Responsible Companies

Creating an ethical portfolio doesn't have to be difficult or intimidating. As long as you know the values that are important to you, you can start using your investment dollars for good. It may be helpful to specifically write down what you're looking for in a socially and environmentally responsible company.

Are gun manufacturers a deal-breaker? Would you be comfortable owning stock in a company that scores lower in the environmental category if it had a majority-female board of directors? Knowing what industries you are and aren't OK with supporting will make it easier to include or exclude certain investments.

Afterward, you want to check out the different ways to invest in these types of companies, and then decide which aligns with your investment goals. Here we go:

- **Specialized funds:** Many investment funds specialize in socially and environmentally responsible investing, also known as "sustainable" or "ESG" (environmental, social, and governance) investing. These funds invest in companies that meet certain standards for social and environmental responsibility, such as reducing greenhouse gas emissions or promoting diversity and inclusion.

- **Individual stocks:** Investors can also consider investing in individual stocks of companies with strong social and environmental responsibility records. Some resources to help identify these companies include rankings and ratings from organizations such as MSCI, Sustainalytics, and the Dow Jones Sustainability Index.

- **Impact investing:** Impact investing is a type of socially and environmentally responsible investing approach that focuses specifically on investments that aim to generate positive social or environmental impact, in addition to financial returns. Examples of impact investing include investing in renewable energy or affordable housing projects.

- **Engaging with companies:** As a shareholder, investors have the ability to engage with the companies they own and advocate for change. This can include participating in shareholder meetings and voting on issues related to social and environmental responsibility, or using tools such as proxy voting to express their views on these issues. Note that this depends on which companies you invest in and the kinds of stock you buy. Not every company stock entitles you to have a say in a company's affairs as they pertain to social and environmental responsibility.

You can as well consider using screens or filters to select companies that meet certain social and environmental criteria.

The next part of this book will shift focus to the quantitative factors of fundamental analysis, starting with financial statement analysis. We'll delve into the various components of financial statements and how to use them to evaluate a company's financial performance.

Key Takeaways

- Responsible investing, also known as socially responsible investing, involves investing money in companies and funds that positively impact society.
- Measuring a company's social and environmental impact is crucial in evaluating the attainment of sustainable objectives.
- When analyzing a sustainability report, you should look for information on a company's environmental and social impact, governance practices, and stakeholder engagement.

Chapter 11

The Balance Sheet Blues: Deciphering Financial Statements

"Given a 10% chance of a 100 times payoff, you should take that bet every time."
— *Jeff Bezos*

Financial statements hold a wealth of information for investors, but deciphering them can be a challenge.

Financial statements are an important tool for business owners. They provide critical information about a company's success by providing a snapshot of its finances. They also serve as the foundation for charting a company's future trajectory.

As an investor, you want to use the financial statements of a company to assess the health and liquidity of its business and make the right decisions regarding your investments.

This chapter covers the use of financial statements in fundamental analysis. It explains how to read and interpret financial statements and covers the key ratios and metrics used to analyze a company's financial performance.

Introduction to Financial Statements

Financial statements provide a snapshot of a company's financial health at a specific point in time. They include key information on what a company owns and owes and how much money it has made and spent. The following are the elements included in a financial statement:

- **Balance sheet:** A balance sheet is a summary of a company's financial position at the end of a specific period, which shows what the company owns and owes. The balance sheet is based on the equation: Assets = Liabilities + Shareholders' Equity.

- **Income statement:** An income statement, also called a profit and loss statement or earnings statement, summarizes a company's revenue and expenses over a specific period. The income statement helps to determine the profitability of the business.

- **Statement of cash flows:** A cash flow statement, also known as a statement of changes in financial position, provides information about how cash moves in and out of the company during a specific period.
- **Statement of shareholders' equity:** A statement of retained earnings reflects the cumulative earnings of the company after accounting for any dividends or distributions made to shareholders. It shows how much the company has retained in earnings and how much has been paid out to shareholders.

Financial statements provide information about a company's **assets, liabilities, revenues, expenses, and profitability**. They can help you, as an investor, to understand a company's financial performance, assess its risk profile, and make informed investment decisions.

The Balance Sheet

When evaluating a company or investment opportunity, fundamental analysts often begin by examining the balance sheet. This financial statement provides a snapshot of a company's assets, liabilities, and equity at a specific point in time, and contains important information for understanding the solvency and operations of a company.

While the balance sheet has many important aspects, certain items may be particularly significant for gaining a general understanding of a company's financial situation. Balance sheets are crucial in various situations, including when a merger is being considered, when a company needs to evaluate asset liquidation to manage debt, when an investor is considering an investment in a company, or when a company is assessing its financial stability for expansion or debt repayment.

In essence, the balance sheet provides important information about a company's financial position and solvency. It can help investors to understand a company's ability to meet its financial obligations and pay its debts.

The two big categories on any balance sheet are assets and liabilities. Assets are resources owned by the company, such as cash, inventory, and property, while liabilities are obligations or debts the company owes, such as loans and accounts payable.

We've also got "owners' equity" as part of the balance sheet, and it represents the residual ownership interest in the company and is calculated by subtracting liabilities from assets.

When evaluating a company's financial performance using the balance sheet, there are several key guidelines that you should follow:

- **Check the company's liquidity**: This refers to the company's ability to meet its short-term financial obligations. One way to assess liquidity is by examining the company's current ratio, which is calculated by dividing current assets by current liabilities. A current ratio of 1 or higher is generally considered to be a good indicator of liquidity.

- **Assess the company's debt levels**: High levels of debt can be a red flag for investors, as it can lead to financial instability and reduced profitability. To assess a company's debt levels, investors can examine its debt-to-equity ratio, which is calculated by dividing total debt by shareholder equity. A lower debt-to-equity ratio is generally preferable, as it suggests that the company is relying less on debt to finance its operations.

- **Evaluate the company's asset utilization**: This refers to how effectively the company uses its assets to generate profits. One way to assess asset utilization is by examining the company's asset turnover ratio, which is calculated by dividing sales by total assets. A higher asset turnover ratio is generally considered to be a positive indicator, as it suggests that the company is generating more revenue per dollar of assets.

- **Check the company's cash position**: This refers to the amount of cash the company has on hand to meet its financial obligations. Investors can examine the company's cash and cash equivalents on the balance sheet to understand its cash position. A company with a healthy cash position is generally considered to be in a better position to weather financial challenges.

- **Compare the company's financial performance over time**: It's important to look at a company's balance sheet over time to get an idea of its financial trends. This can involve comparing key financial ratios and metrics from year to year, as well as examining any significant changes in the company's financial position.

By following these guidelines, you can gain a better understanding of a company's financial performance using the balance sheet and use this information to make informed investment decisions.

The Income Statement

An income statement shows a company's financial performance over a period of time, typically one year. The income statement includes revenue, which is

The Balance Sheet Blues: Deciphering Financial Statements

the money that a company earns from its operations, and expenses, which are the costs associated with generating that revenue.

The difference between revenue and expenses is the company's net income, which can be either positive (profit) or negative (loss). By looking at the income statement, investors can get an idea of a company's profitability and financial performance over time.

Here are guidelines for evaluating a company's financial performance using the income statement:

- **Compare net income to previous periods to see if the company is improving or declining:** By looking at a company's net income over a period of time, you can get an idea of its overall financial health. A consistent increase in net income is generally a positive sign, while a decline in net income could be cause for concern.

- **Compare net income to the company's industry average to see if the company is outperforming or underperforming:** It's important to understand how a company's net income compares to its industry peers. A company that is consistently outperforming its competitors may be a good investment opportunity.

- **Look at the company's gross margin, which is the percentage of revenue that remains after accounting for the cost of goods sold:** A high gross margin indicates that the company is able to sell its products at a markup, which is a good sign for investors.

- **Examine the company's operating expenses, such as selling and administrative expenses, to see if they align with industry averages:** If a company's operating expenses are higher than its peers, it may be an indication that the company is not operating efficiently.

- **Look at the company's bottom line, which is the net income after accounting for taxes and other items:** A company's bottom line is a good indicator of its overall profitability.

- **Evaluate the company's earnings per share (EPS), which is net income divided by the number of outstanding shares of stock. A higher EPS is generally considered to be more favorable for investors:** A higher EPS indicates that the company is generating more profits per share, which can make it more attractive to investors.

As an investor, you want to check for the revenue from selling products or services, expenses to generate the revenue and manage your business, and net income (or profit) that remains after your expenses.

The Cash Flow Statement

A cash flow statement shows the inflow and outflow of cash for a company over a period of time, typically one year. The cash flow statement is used to understand a company's financial health and ability to generate cash.

The cash flow statement is divided into three main sections: operating activities, investing activities, and financing activities. Operating activities include the cash generated from a company's daily operations, such as the sale of goods or services; investing activities include the cash used for long-term investments, such as purchasing equipment or real estate; and financing activities include the cash generated or used from financing sources, such as issuing bonds or taking out loans.

By looking at the cash flow statement, you can get an idea of a company's financial stability and ability to generate cash. Below are guidelines for evaluating a company's financial performance using the cash flow statement:

- **Look at the company's net cash flow from operating activities, which indicates the company's ability to generate cash from its everyday business operations:** Positive operating cash flow is generally seen as a good sign, as it shows that the company is able to generate cash from its core operations.

- **Examine the company's net cash flow from investing activities, which shows the company's use of cash for investments in long-term assets, such as property, plant, and equipment:** This can provide insight into the company's growth prospects and its ability to make capital expenditures.

- **Analyze the company's net cash flow from financing activities, which reveals the company's use of cash to fund its operations, such as through borrowing or issuing equity:** This can provide insight into the company's financing activities and its ability to raise capital.

- **Compare the company's net cash flow from operating activities to its net income, which can provide insight into the company's overall financial health:** If a company's net income is significantly higher than its operating cash flow, it may be a red flag that the company is not generating enough cash from its operations.

- **Evaluate the company's overall cash position and cash flow trends over time to determine if it is generating enough cash to support its operations and future growth:** A company that consistently generates positive cash flow and has a strong cash position is generally seen as a good investment.

Overall, the financial statement is a critical document that provides a snapshot of a company's financial position.

Meanwhile, ratio analysis is another tool investors can use to evaluate a company's financial performance. In the next chapter, we'll discuss the various types of ratios and how to use them to make informed investment decisions.

Key Takeaways

- Financial statements provide critical information about a company's success by providing a snapshot of its finances.
- Investors use the financial statements of a company to assess the health and liquidity of its business and make the right decisions regarding their investments.
- Financial statements include four main elements: balance sheet, income statement, statement of cash flows, and statement of shareholder's equity.

Chapter 12

Ratio Analysis: Using Numbers to Evaluate a Company's Performance

"Wealth is a ratio, not a number."
— *Alex Hormozi*

Alex Hormozi's quote above suggests that when evaluating a company's financial health or potential for investment, it is not the absolute value of their financial figures that matter, but rather the ratios and relationships between those figures.

For example, a company with $1 billion in assets may seem impressive, but if they have $2 billion in liabilities, its financial health may be poor. On the other hand, a company with $100 million in assets and $50 million in liabilities may be more financially stable. Got it?

By looking at ratios such as liquidity ratios, profitability ratios, debt ratios, and efficiency ratios, you can better understand a company's financial performance and potential for growth.

In this chapter, we will look at the use of ratios in fundamental analysis. It covers the different types of ratios used to evaluate a company's financial performance and explains how to interpret and use these ratios to make informed investment decisions.

Introduction to Ratio Analysis

Ratio analysis is a tool that investors can use to evaluate a company's financial performance by comparing different financial metrics to each other. There are various types of ratios that can be used, including **liquidity ratios, profitability ratios, debt ratios, and efficiency ratios.** We will look into each of these ratios in the subsequent sections.

Ratio analysis can provide investors with valuable insights into a company's financial health and help them make informed investment decisions. When using ratio analysis, it is important to consider the company's industry and compare its ratios to those of its peers or industry averages.

Investors should also be aware that ratios can be affected by a variety of factors, such as the company's size, growth rate, and business model, and should be used in conjunction with other analysis techniques.

Liquidity Ratios

Liquidity ratios measure a company's ability to pay its short-term debts and obligations. Two common liquidity ratios are the current ratio and the quick ratio.

We can calculate the current ratio by dividing current assets by current liabilities. This ratio measures a company's ability to pay its short-term obligations using its current assets. A current ratio of 1.5 or higher is generally considered to be healthy, although this can vary depending on the industry and the company's business model.

A higher current ratio is generally considered better, as it indicates that the company has enough current assets to cover its current liabilities. However, a very high current ratio could mean that the company is not efficiently using its current assets to generate revenue.

Also referred to as the acid-test ratio, the quick ratio is a more conservative measure of a company's ability to meet its short-term obligations. This ratio excludes inventory from current assets, as inventory can be difficult to convert to cash quickly. The quick ratio is calculated by dividing quick assets (current assets minus inventory) by current liabilities.

A quick ratio of 1.0 or higher is also generally considered to be healthy. A higher quick ratio is generally considered better, as it indicates that the company can cover its current liabilities without relying on inventory.

By looking at liquidity ratios, investors can get an idea of a company's financial flexibility and ability to meet its short-term obligations.

Profitability Ratios

Profitability ratios measure a company's ability to generate profits from its operations. Some common profitability ratios include the return on investment (ROI), which measures the profitability of a company's assets, and the gross profit margin, which measures the percentage of sales that exceeds the cost of goods sold.

A ROI of 15% or higher is generally considered to be good, although this can vary depending on the industry and the company's business model. Meanwhile, a gross profit margin of 40% or higher is generally considered to be healthy, although this can also vary depending on the industry and the company's business model.

By looking at profitability ratios, investors can get an idea of a company's efficiency and ability to generate profits.

Debt Ratios

Debt ratios measure a company's level of debt and its ability to manage that debt. Some common debt ratios include the debt-to-equity ratio, which compares a company's total debt to its shareholder equity, and the interest coverage ratio, which measures a company's ability to pay its interest expenses.

By looking at debt ratios, investors can get an idea of a company's financial leverage and risk level. Below are guidelines for evaluating a company's debt ratios:

- **Debt-to-equity ratio**: This ratio measures the amount of debt a company has in relation to its equity. A ratio of less than 1 suggests that the company has more equity than debt, which may indicate a stronger financial position. A ratio of more than 1 suggests that the company has more debt than equity, which may indicate a riskier financial position.

The formula for calculating the debt-to-equity ratio is:

$$Debt-to-equity\ ratio = \frac{Total\ debt}{Total\ equity}$$

- **Interest coverage ratio**: This ratio measures a company's ability to cover its interest expenses with its earnings. A ratio of more than 1 suggests that the company is generating sufficient income to cover its interest expenses, while a ratio of less than 1 may indicate financial distress.

The formula for calculating the interest coverage ratio is:

$$Interest\ coverage\ ratio = \frac{Earnings\ before\ interest\ and\ taxes\ (EBIT)}{Interest\ expense}$$

By evaluating a company's debt ratios, you can gain insights into the company's financial health and its ability to manage its debt obligations. However, it's important to consider these ratios in the context of the industry and market conditions, as well as other factors like the company's growth prospects and management team.

Efficiency Ratios

Efficiency ratios measure a company's ability to use its assets and resources efficiently to generate sales and profits. Some common efficiency ratios include the inventory turnover ratio, which measures how quickly a company can sell its inventory, and the asset turnover ratio, which measures a company's ability to generate sales from its assets.

By looking at efficiency ratios, investors can get an idea of a company's management effectiveness and efficiency in using its resources. Here are guidelines for evaluating a company's efficiency ratios:

- **Inventory Turnover Ratio**: The inventory turnover ratio measures how many times a company sells and replaces its inventory over a specific period of time. A high inventory turnover ratio suggests that the company is efficiently managing its inventory and may be in a strong financial position, while a low inventory turnover ratio may indicate that the company is struggling to sell its inventory and may be in a weaker financial position.

The inventory turnover ratio is calculated as follows:

$$\text{Inventory Turnover Ratio} = \frac{\text{Cost of Goods Sold}}{\text{Average Inventory}}$$

- **Asset Turnover Ratio**: The asset turnover ratio measures how effectively a company is using its assets to generate sales. A high asset turnover ratio suggests that the company is effectively using its assets to generate sales and may be in a strong financial position, while a low asset turnover ratio may indicate that the company is not using its assets efficiently and may be in a weaker financial position.

The asset turnover ratio is calculated as follows:

$$\text{Asset Turnover Ratio} = \frac{\text{Revenue}}{\text{Average Total Assets}}$$

In summary, it is important to analyze a company's efficiency ratios to determine how well it is managing its inventory and how effectively it is using its assets to generate sales. A high inventory turnover ratio and a high asset turnover ratio indicate that a company is efficiently managing its resources and may be in a strong financial position, while a low turnover ratio suggests the opposite.

In addition to analyzing a company's past financial performance, investors can also use financial forecasting and projections to get a sense of how a company is likely to perform in the future. In the next chapter, we'll discuss the process for creating financial forecasts and the key factors to consider.

Key Takeaways

- By looking at ratios such as liquidity ratios, profitability ratios, debt ratios, and efficiency ratios, you can better understand a company's financial performance and potential for growth.

- Ratio analysis can provide investors with valuable insights into a company's financial health and help them to make informed investment decisions.

- Liquidity ratios measure a company's ability to pay its short-term debts and obligations.

- By looking at profitability ratios, investors can get an idea of a company's efficiency and ability to generate profits.

- By evaluating a company's debt ratios, you can gain insights into the company's financial health and its ability to manage its debt obligations.

- Efficiency ratios measure a company's ability to use its assets and resources efficiently to generate sales and profits.

Chapter 13

Peering Into the Future: Using Financial Forecasts and Projections in Fundamental Analysis

"Know what you own, and know why you own it."
— Peter Lynch

What if you could get a sneak peek into the future?

Financial forecasting and projections can give you an idea of what might be coming and help inform your investment decisions. Learn how to use them effectively in this chapter.

This chapter will explore the use of financial forecasting and projections in fundamental analysis. We will look into the different methods and approaches that can be used to forecast a company's financial performance and cover the key considerations and pitfalls to be aware of when making financial projections.

Introduction to Financial Forecasts and Projections

Financial forecasts and projections are estimates of a company's future financial performance based on analysis of its past and current financial data and industry trends. There are various types of financial forecasts and projections that can be made, including:

- **Sales forecasts**: These predict the amount of revenue a company is expected to generate in the future. Sales forecasts are typically based on historical sales data, market trends, and other factors that may impact sales. For example, you can use sales forecasts to predict the demand for a company's new product or to project sales growth over the next several years.

- **Earnings projections**: These estimates predict a company's future earnings, which are calculated by subtracting expenses from revenue. Earnings projections can provide insight into a company's profitability and overall financial health. For example, as an analyst, you can use earnings projections to evaluate a company's ability to generate profits over the next several years.

- **Cash flow forecasts**: These forecasts the amount of cash a company is expected to generate or use in the future. Cash flow forecasts can provide insight into a company's ability to pay its bills, fund operations, and invest in future growth opportunities. For example, you can use a company's cash flow forecasts to plan for future capital expenditures or determine how much debt it can afford to take on.

In theory, failing to undertake regular financial forecasting leaves you flying blind. Frequent forecasting has numerous advantages for some of the company's most important processes. You need it to understand a company's potential future performance and make informed investment decisions.

Preparing Financial Forecasts and Projections

The process of creating financial forecasts and projections involves analyzing a company's past and current financial data, as well as industry trends and economic conditions. Here's how to go about it:

- Gather relevant financial data, including past financial statements and industry trends.
- Determine the key drivers of the company's financial performance, such as sales growth, cost of goods sold, and operating expenses.
- Analyze the economic and market conditions that may impact the company's financial performance.
- Use financial modeling tools and techniques to project future financial performance based on the gathered data and analysis.
- Review and refine the financial forecasts and projections as needed.

Some key factors to consider when creating financial forecasts and projections include the company's growth rate, market demand, competitive environment, and economic conditions.

To create accurate financial forecasts and projections, it is important to use reliable sources of information and to be mindful of potential biases or assumptions. To find data for financial forecasts and projections, consider the following sources:

- The company's past financial statements, which can provide insight into historical performance and trends.

- Industry reports and market research, which can provide information on industry trends and competitive environment.
- Economic data and forecasts, which can provide information on macroeconomic conditions and their potential impact on the company's performance.

Meanwhile, the following are methods for creating financial forecasts and projections:

- **Historical analysis:** This method involves analyzing the company's past financial performance and using it to project future performance. It assumes that the future will be similar to the past. Historical analysis involves examining financial statements, such as income statements, balance sheets, and cash flow statements, to identify trends and patterns. For example, you can analyze a company's revenue growth rate over the past five years to project its future revenue growth rate.
- **Bottom-up analysis**: This method involves analyzing the company's individual components, such as its sales and expenses, and using them to project future performance. It assumes that a company's future financial performance is a function of its individual components. Bottom-up analysis involves breaking down a company's financial statements into smaller parts and analyzing each part individually. For example, you can analyze a company's sales growth rate, cost of goods sold, and operating expenses to project its future profitability.
- **Top-down analysis**: This method involves analyzing macroeconomic conditions and using them to project the company's future performance. It assumes that the broader economic environment affects a company's financial performance. Top-down analysis involves examining economic indicators, such as GDP growth rate, inflation rate, and interest rates, to predict how they will impact the company's financial performance. For example, you can analyze the economic conditions of a country where a company operates to project its future revenue growth rate.

And if you are looking to find financial forecasts and projections made by other analysts, consider the following sources:

- **Investment research firms**: Many investment research firms provide financial forecasts and projections for companies as part of their research services.
- **Financial news and media outlets**: Some financial news and media outlets provide financial forecasts and projections for companies as part of their coverage.

- **Analyst reports**: Many analysts who cover specific companies or industries provide financial forecasts and projections in their reports.

Evaluating Financial Forecasts and Projections

When evaluating financial forecasts and projections, investors should consider several key factors to determine their reliability and usefulness. These factors include:

- **Credibility of the source**: The credibility of the source of the financial forecast is an important consideration. Investors should look for forecasts and projections from reputable sources such as established analysts or financial institutions. In addition, the track record of the source in making accurate forecasts and projections should be considered.

- **The assumptions used**: The assumptions used in the financial forecast or projection should be carefully examined. Investors should understand the underlying assumptions and consider whether they are reasonable and realistic. They should also evaluate the impact of changes to the assumptions on the forecast or projection.

- **The track record of the company or analyst making the forecast**: This should also be considered. Investors should look for a history of accurate forecasts and projections and consider the reasons for any past errors.

Investors should also consider the level of uncertainty and risk inherent in financial forecasts and projections and how that may impact their investment decisions.

By thoroughly evaluating financial forecasts and projections, investors can make more informed and confident investment decisions based on a company's potential future performance.

Now that we've covered the qualitative and quantitative factors of fundamental analysis, it's time to move on to valuation. In the next chapter, we'll discuss the different approaches you can take to assess a company's worth.

Key Takeaways

- Financial forecasts and projections are estimates of a company's future financial performance.
- The process for creating financial forecasts and projections is based on analysis of a company's past and current financial data and industry trends.
- The key factors an investor should consider when evaluating financial forecasts and projections include the credibility of the source, the assumptions used, and the track record of the company or analyst making the forecast.

Chapter 14
The Art of Valuation: Different Approaches to Assessing a Company's Worth

"In the short run, the market is a voting machine but in the long run, it is a weighing machine."
— Benjamin Graham

This Benjamin Graham's quote above explains the difference between short-term market fluctuations and the long-term intrinsic value of a company.

In the short run, the market can be volatile and driven by emotions and perceptions, which can cause the stock prices to fluctuate wildly based on the prevailing sentiments among investors. This can cause the stock to be overvalued or undervalued in the short term, based on investors' sentiments, news, rumors, or other factors.

However, in the long run, the market tends to reflect the underlying intrinsic value of a company. The true value of a company is based on its fundamentals such as earnings, growth potential, management quality, and other factors that can be analyzed through fundamental analysis.

Over time, the market tends to recognize and reflect these underlying fundamentals, leading to a more stable and accurate valuation of the company. This is why Graham referred to the market as a *"weighing machine"* in the long run, as it is more focused on the true value of the company rather than short-term fluctuations.

This chapter covers the different methods investors can use to value a company in fundamental analysis. It explains the key considerations and assumptions involved in each method and provides guidance on how to choose the most appropriate method for a given situation.

Introduction to Valuation

If you are willing to beat the market as an investor, then you must master the skill of stock valuation. Essentially, stock valuation is the process of determining the fair value or worth of a company or asset.

The significance of stock valuation stems from the fact that a stock's intrinsic value may differ from its present price. An investor can assess whether a stock is over or undervalued at its current market price by knowing its intrinsic value.

There are various approaches to valuation, including intrinsic valuation, relative valuation, and discounted cash flow analysis. And we will explore each in detail in subsequent sections of this chapter.

But typically, factors that can influence a company's value include its financial performance, growth prospects, market conditions, and risk profile.

Intrinsic Valuation

Intrinsic valuation is a technique that estimates the intrinsic or true value of a company or asset based on its fundamental characteristics. Some common intrinsic valuation techniques include the **discounted cash flow (DCF) method**, which estimates the present value of a company's future cash flows, and the **net asset value (NAV) method**, which estimates the value of a company based on its net assets.

Intrinsic valuation can provide investors with a benchmark for evaluating a company's value and can help them to identify undervalued or overvalued investments.

Here's how to use this method to evaluate a company's financials:

- **Financial statements:** Investors should carefully examine the company's balance sheets, income statements, and cash flow statements to determine its current financial health and performance. This includes evaluating the company's revenue growth, profit margins, cash flow generation, and overall financial stability.

- **Growth potential:** In addition to evaluating a company's current financials, investors should also consider the company's growth potential and the prospects for its industry or sector. This involves analyzing market trends, competition, and the company's overall business strategy to determine its ability to grow and generate future earnings.

- **Management team:** A company's management team can significantly impact its long-term success. Investors should evaluate the company's leadership, experience, and track record to determine the management team's quality and ability to execute the company's business strategy.

- **Competitive advantage**: Investors should also consider the company's competitive advantage and unique value proposition. This involves analyzing the company's products or services and its brand and reputation to determine how it differentiates itself from competitors and how sustainable that differentiation is.

By considering these factors, you can, as an investor, use intrinsic valuation to estimate a company's true worth and determine whether its current market price is overvalued or undervalued.

Relative Valuation

Relative valuation is a technique that compares a company's value to that of its peers or market benchmarks. Some common relative valuation techniques include the price-to-earnings (P/E) ratio, which compares a company's share price to its earnings per share, and the price-to-book (P/B) ratio, which compares a company's share price to its book value.

Relative valuation can provide investors with a frame of reference when evaluating a company's value relative to its peers or market benchmarks. Here's how to use this method to evaluate a company's financials:

- **Identify comparable companies**: First, you need to identify comparable companies in the same industry or sector as the company you are evaluating. This will help you establish industry benchmarks for financial metrics.

- **Choose relevant financial metrics**: Next, you need to select financial metrics relevant to the industry or sector in which the company operates. Some common metrics include price-to-earnings ratio (P/E ratio), price-to-book ratio (P/B ratio), and price-to-sales ratio (P/S ratio).

- **Calculate the financial metrics**: Once you have identified the comparable companies and relevant financial metrics, you can calculate the metrics for each company.

- **Compare the metrics**: Compare the financial metrics of the company you are evaluating to those of the comparable companies or industry benchmarks. If the company's metrics are higher than the industry average, it may be overvalued, and if they are lower, it may be undervalued.

- **Consider other factors**: Finally, you should consider other factors that may impact the company's valuation, such as its market position, growth prospects, and macroeconomic conditions. This will help you get a more complete picture of the company's financial health and performance.

Discounted Cash Flow Analysis

Discounted cash flow (DCF) analysis is a technique that estimates the present value of a company's future cash flows. A DCF analysis includes a discount rate, which is the required rate of return used to discount the future cash flows, and a terminal value, which is the estimated value of the company beyond the forecast period

DCF analysis can provide investors with a benchmark for evaluating a company's value and can help them to identify undervalued or overvalued investments. Here's how to use this method to evaluate a company's financials:

1. **Estimate future cash flows**: The first step in DCF analysis is to estimate the company's future cash flows. This involves making assumptions about the company's revenue growth, profit margins, capital expenditures, and working capital requirements.
2. **Discount cash flows to present value**: Once future cash flows are estimated, they are then discounted to present value using an appropriate discount rate. The discount rate should reflect the risk associated with the investment and the time value of money.
3. **Consider growth prospects and risks**: DCF analysis requires the consideration of a company's growth prospects and the risks involved in achieving those cash flows. For instance, if a company operates in a highly competitive industry with high barriers to entry, it may be riskier and require a higher discount rate.
4. **Analyze financial statements**: A thorough analysis of the company's financial statements is necessary when using DCF analysis. Thee company's profitability, efficiency, and financial leverage are important factors to consider.
5. **Compare intrinsic value to market price**: The final step in DCF analysis is to compare the estimated intrinsic value to the current market price of the company's stock. If the intrinsic value is higher than the market price, the company may be undervalued, indicating a potential buying opportunity. If the intrinsic value is lower than the market price, the company may be overvalued, indicating that the stock is not a good investment at the current price.

In summary, DCF analysis is a method of valuing a company based on its future cash flows, discounting them to present value, and comparing the resulting intrinsic value to the company's market price.

As you can see, we've covered a lot of information in the preceding chapters. And so, in this next and last chapter, we'll bring it all together and walk through the process of using fundamental analysis to make investment decisions.

Key Takeaways

- If you are willing to beat the market as an investor, then you must master the skill of stock valuation.
- Intrinsic valuation is a technique that estimates the intrinsic or true value of a company or asset based on its fundamental characteristics.
- Relative valuation is a technique that compares a company's value to that of its peers or market benchmarks.
- Discounted cash flow (DCF) analysis is a technique that estimates the present value of a company's future cash flows.

Chapter 15

Putting it all Together: Using Fundamental Analysis to Make Investment Decisions

"Behind every stock is a company. Find out what it's doing."
— Peter Lynch

I couldn't have agreed more with Peter Lynch's quote; it pretty much highlights the importance of understanding a company's business operations when evaluating its investment potential.

Let's say, for instance, you are passionate about the environment and social responsibility. So you decide to invest in a company called SolarCity, a provider of solar power systems for homes and businesses. You are attracted to the company's mission of promoting clean energy and reducing carbon emissions, but you also want to make sure it is a good investment.

So you do your research on SolarCity, looking beyond the stock price and financial statements to understand the company's business model and growth potential. Then you learn that the company offers a unique leasing program that allows customers to install solar panels without paying the high upfront costs. SolarCity would install the panels, maintain them, and customers would pay a monthly fee for the energy they produced.

Then you find out that the company is expanding rapidly and has signed agreements with major corporations and governments to provide solar energy solutions. You also learned about the leadership team, including the founder and CEO, who have a strong track record of success in the solar industry.

Based on your research, you decide to invest in SolarCity. Your due diligence and understanding of the company's operations and mission gives you confidence in your investment decision. Over time, SolarCity continues to grow and is eventually acquired by Tesla, resulting in a profitable return on your investment.

You get it now?

That's exactly how going beyond the stock price and financial statements to understand the company's business and industry can guide you in making informed decisions. Not only will you learn about the company's financials but also its growth potential, leadership team, and mission.

And so, we've put together this final chapter to help you integrate all the lessons we've covered from the preceding chapters by practically walking you through various examples of using fundamental analysis to assess different companies' stocks.

Example #1: The Coca-Cola Company

The Coca-Cola Company is one great example we can use fundamental analysis for. Here is what the process of using fundamental analysis to assess Coca-Cola stock (NYSE: KO) would look like:

Step 1: Study the industry and its competitors

The first step in evaluating Coca-Cola is to study the beverage industry and its competitors. We can do this by examining the economy across various reports, using published statistics metrics like the consumer price index (an inflation measure), GDP growth, exports/imports, and interest rates.

Then, our focus should shift to the competitor companies in the industry. For example, PepsiCo, Dr. Pepper Snapple Group, and Nestle are all major competitors to Coca-Cola.

Understanding the industry trends, market share, and competitive landscape will help us evaluate Coca-Cola's strengths and weaknesses.

Step 2: Understand the company and its business

The next step is to gather as much information as possible about Coca-Cola from the Coca-Cola company or the Security and Exchange Commission's Edgar filings database. Our focus will include understanding Coca-Cola's business model and how the company generates revenue.

Coca-Cola's main revenue source is from selling non-alcoholic beverages, including sparkling soft drinks, water, sports drinks, and teas. The company also earns revenue from licensing its products and brands.

Additionally, it's important to review the company's financial statements, annual reports, investor presentations, conference calls, and news articles.

We can also use an independent digital financial media firm like CSIMarket to gather our data. Because CSIMarket provides fundamental research data for investors, we can start by checking the worth of the company's assets, income streams, debts, and liabilities. Comparisons of objective indicators such as revenue, earnings, and growth may be found, particularly in the context of the broader beverage business.

Step 3: Analyze the financials

One of the most important aspects of fundamental analysis is analyzing the financials of a company. This includes looking at metrics such as Earnings Per Share (EPS), Price-to-Earnings (P/E) Ratio, Debt to Equity, Return on Equity (ROE), and free cash flow.

For Coca-Cola, we would want to see consistent revenue and earnings growth, a healthy P/E ratio compared to its industry peers, and a manageable debt-to-equity ratio. Other factors to consider include dividend payments, which Coca-Cola has a long history of paying to its shareholders, and the company's cash reserves. Doing so will enable us to compare growth rates to the industry and sector Coca-Cola operates in to see if the company is valued correctly.

For example, according to Investopedia, here's what the possible ratios and metrics of Coca-Cola looks like for August 2021 to August 2022:

	Coca-Cola	Industry	Sector
Y/Y Revenue Growth	13.48%	10.86%	16.18%
P/E Ratio	29.12	25.16	18.68
Price to Free Cash Flow	24	7.45	4.23
Debt to Equity (TTM)	1.57	0.14	0.11
Quick Ratio (TTM)	0.16	0.24	0.2
Return on Equity (TTM)	13.14%	30.21%	23.16%
Return on Assets (TTM)	11.5%	8.69%	7.91%
Return on Investment (TTM)	13.14%	19.76%	15.84%
Revenue per Employee (TTM)	$111,578	$55,015	$66,896

When analyzing a company's performance, it's important to consider factors beyond the numbers and ratios. For instance, Coca-Cola has been in business since 1892, enduring wars, epidemics, stock market crashes, and financial crises. This longevity and resilience are rare qualities in any business.

Step 4: Analyze forecasts/projections

In order to get a sense of Coca-Cola's future growth potential, it's important to analyze the company's forecasts and projections. We can do this by reviewing the company's annual report, investor presentations, conference calls, and news articles.

We can also look at external sources such as industry reports and expert analysis to get a sense of future trends and developments. Key factors to consider include the company's plans for growth, including potential expansion into new markets or product lines, as well as any potential risks or challenges that may impact the company's performance.

Step 5: Put a value on the company and check this against its stock price

Once all the above steps have been completed, we can then proceed to put a value on the company and compare it to its stock price to determine whether it's worth investing in.

It's an easy-peasy process; it comes down to comparing Coca-Cola's financial parameters with its peers in order to find out whether the company has a better growth opportunity or not, or if there is another company in the same sector with a better growth potential in the future. A thorough analysis of Coca-Cola's financials, forecasts, and projections can help investors determine whether the company is undervalued or overvalued, and make an informed investment decision.

In this case, while Coca-Cola has more debt than equity, it generates greater returns using its assets than the rest of the industry. Although it has lower liquidity than other companies, Coca-Cola's net cash flows exceed $1 billion, providing flexibility.

Another useful metric is revenue per employee. Coca-Cola's employees generate twice the revenue of comparable companies, which may be attributed to investments in technology or more efficient systems.

Furthermore, the value of a company's brand can also impact its investment potential. Coca-Cola is a well-established brand with global recognition, which can add value to an investment. Along with growth and an above-average price-to-earnings ratio, good return on investment, and above-industry asset returns, we can consider these factors when evaluating Coca-Cola.

Example #2: Amazon

Amazon is another well-known company we can use fundamental analysis for. Here is what the process of using fundamental analysis to assess Amazon stock (NASDAQ: AMZN) would look like:

Step 1: Study the industry and competitors

To evaluate Amazon's potential as an investment, start by studying the e-commerce industry and its competitors. This involves analyzing the macroeconomic factors that could affect the industry and considering the competitive landscape for Amazon.

In terms of macroeconomic factors, we want to look at metrics such as inflation, GDP growth, and interest rates, which can impact consumer spending patterns. When it comes to competitors, examine Amazon's direct competitors, such as Walmart, eBay, etc., as well as other companies that may compete with Amazon in specific areas, such as Alphabet, Microsoft, Facebook, etc.

Step 2: Understand the company and its business

Next, we want to gather information about Amazon's business, including its history, operations, products and services, and growth potential. You can find this information in the company's annual report, investor presentations, and news releases.

As seen in the chart below, Amazon has shown considerable revenue growth since 2004:

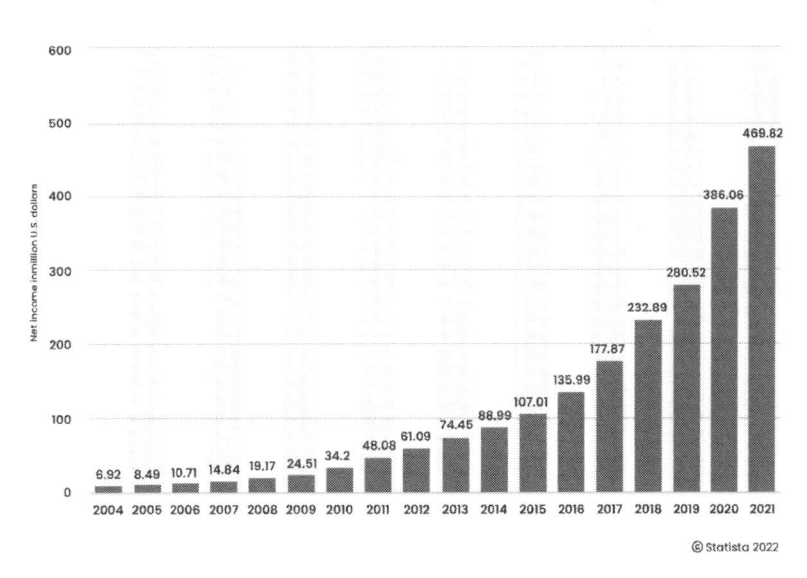

Year	Net Income (million U.S. dollars)
2004	6.92
2005	8.49
2006	10.71
2007	14.84
2008	19.17
2009	24.51
2010	34.2
2011	48.08
2012	61.09
2013	74.45
2014	88.99
2015	107.01
2016	135.99
2017	177.87
2018	232.89
2019	280.52
2020	386.06
2021	469.82

© Statista 2022

Fundamental Analysis Essentials

Understanding Amazon's business and strategy is important to identify the opportunities and risks associated with the investment.

Step 3: Analyze the financials

After understanding Amazon's business, we need to analyze its financial statements. We want to look at metrics such as earnings per share, P/E ratio, P/B ratio, return on equity, and profit margin. These financial ratios can help us determine whether the company is profitable and efficiently using its assets to generate returns for shareholders.

As the chart below illustrates, Amazon's earnings only began to rise significantly since 2015:

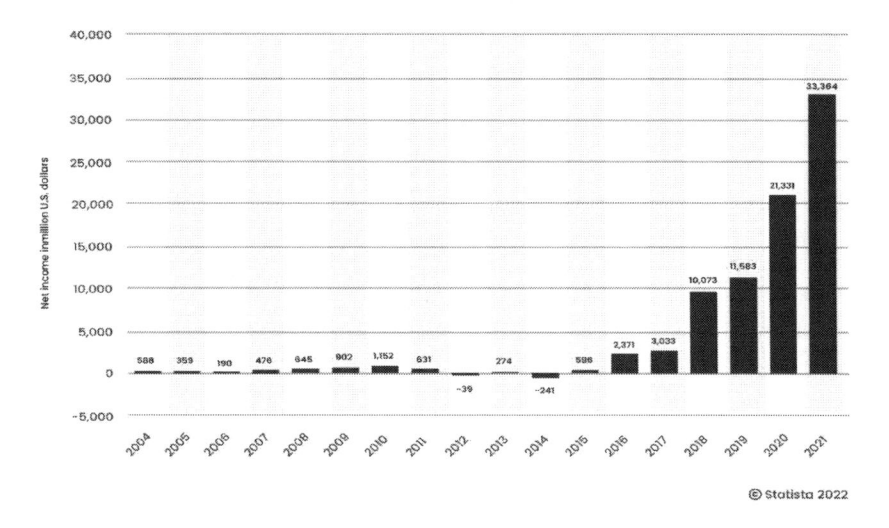

Another critical underlying factor is that Amazon has outperformed consensus Earnings projections in two of the last four quarters.

Earnings Per Share

● ESTIMATED   ● REPORTED

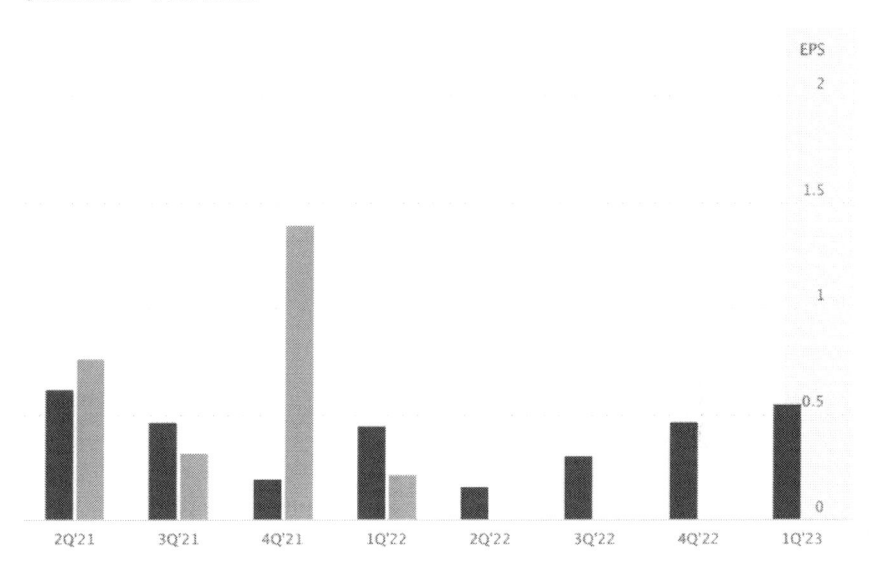

[Bar chart showing EPS estimated vs reported from 2Q'21 through 1Q'23, with y-axis ranging from 0 to 2]

Such earnings data shows that Amazon is healthy and aims for growth that beats expectations every year. The best news is that they are succeeding, for now, at least.

For our analysis, we will be using 2020/22 data so we can have a better idea of what the process looks like. Here's what the numbers look like for Amazon:

Amazon has a diluted earnings per share: $2.07

P/E ratio: 59.05

P/B ratio: 9.30

ROE: 28.8% as of December 2021

It's worth noting that despite Amazon's current stock price of $120.73, its diluted EPS appears relatively low, resulting in an exceptionally high P/E ratio. This is typical for a leading IT company like Amazon, as they continuously invest in research and development to fuel their growth. Consequently, the P/E ratio indicates that only a small portion of Amazon's earnings is paid out to shareholders.

In terms of the P/B ratio, which is calculated by dividing Amazon's stock price of $120.09 by its book value per share of $13.18 for the quarter ending in 2022, a ratio of nearly 10 is unusually high. This indicates that investors are

119

currently paying almost ten times more for an Amazon share than the book value of the company.

Step 4: Analyze forecasts/projections

Once you have evaluated Amazon's current financials, we want to check the company's forecasts and projections for the future. This information can be found in the company's annual report, investor presentations, and conference calls. Look at the company's growth strategy, new product and service offerings, and plans for international expansion.

Amazon, in this case, is currently making significant efforts in fields such as robotization and artificial intelligence, which are actively being pursued through considerable research and development investments. As a result, there is little left for the shareholders in terms of earnings.

However, this indicates that Amazon is focused on expansion and growth, which is likely to lead to an increase in its stock price. Over the past four years, Amazon's stock price has risen by an average of more than 40%, suggesting that this strategy has been effective in driving the company's growth.

Step 5: Put a value on the company and check this against its stock price

After analyzing the financials and forecasts, we can then determine the intrinsic value of Amazon. We simply compare the company's financial parameters with those of its peers in the industry to determine its relative value.

Looking at Amazon, the company's ROE% remains high for its sector, although Apple Inc. boasts of an even higher percentage. Here's a general comparison with other top tech companies from the S&P 500:

- Alphabet's (NASDAQ: GOOG) ROE: 11.6%
- Microsoft's (NASDAQ: MSFT) ROE: 23.1%
- Apple's (NASDAQ: AAPL) ROE: 48.7%
- Facebook's (NASDAQ: FB) ROE: 25%

When compared to other major tech firms in the S&P 500, Amazon's ROE% implies that the company is relatively efficient in generating returns on shareholder investment, outperforming four of the five listed firms. It's essential to note that this does not necessarily imply that other firms like Alphabet, Microsoft, Apple, and Facebook are inefficient in generating returns, but rather that they are less efficient than Amazon and Apple.

Example #3: Maruti Suzuki India Limited

In this last example, let's take a look at Maruti Suzuki, an Indian automobile manufacturer, based in New Delhi. Here is what the process of using fundamental analysis to assess Maruti Suzuki stock (NSE: MARUTI) would look like:

Step 1: Study the industry and its competitors

To conduct a fundamental analysis of Maruti Suzuki India, the first step is to evaluate the potential for future growth in the automobile industry. This involves conducting a sector analysis to determine if government policies and economic conditions favor the industry.

Once the outlook for the sector is positive, we can then research the specific company and compare its financial parameters with its peers in the industry.

The goal is to determine whether Maruti Suzuki is poised for better growth opportunities compared to other companies in the same sector, or if there are other companies with better potential for growth in the future.

Additionally, research on the automotive industry and the market share of Maruti Suzuki India compared to its competitors, such as Tata Motors and Mahindra & Mahindra, can help gain a better understanding of the company's position in the market.

Step 2: Understand the company and its business

To understand the company's business and its future growth prospects, you can gather reports about Maruti Suzuki India from various sources, such as its annual reports, investor presentations, and conference calls. You can also study the company's history, its management team, and its mission and vision statements to gain a better understanding of its goals and objectives.

Maruti Suzuki India Limited, headquartered in New Delhi, is an Indian automaker that was founded in 1981 and previously owned by the Indian government until it was sold to Suzuki Motor Corporation in 2003. With a current market share of 42% in the Indian passenger car market as of September 2022, Maruti Suzuki has established itself as a leading player in the industry.

Step 3: Analyze the financials

Analyzing the financials of Maruti Suzuki India can provide insight into the company's past and current performance.

We can analyze financial metrics such as annual dividend payout, earnings per share, price-to-earnings ratio, return on equity, and net profit margin. This analysis will help us understand the company's financial health and ability to generate profits and growth.

Step 4: Analyze forecasts/projections

Using the company's annual report, investor presentations, and conference calls, you can analyze the company's forecasts and projections. This analysis will help you understand the company's growth prospects and future potential.

You can also compare the company's projections with its competitors to get a better idea of the industry's growth potential.

Step 5: Put a value on the company and check this against its stock price

Once you have completed the previous steps, you can put a value on Maruti Suzuki India and compare it to its stock price. The process is similar to those of Examples 1 and 2.

In order to assess the growth potential of Maruti Suzuki and its peers, we need to compare the company's financial parameters to determine if it has a competitive advantage over other companies in the same sector or if other companies offer better growth potential for investment.

And this brings us to the end of this guide.

Key Takeaways

- Going beyond the stock price and financial statements to understand the company's business and industry can guide you in making informed decisions.

- It's important to review the company's financial statements, annual reports, investor presentations, conference calls, and news articles.

- In terms of macroeconomic factors, you want to look at metrics such as inflation, GDP growth, and interest rates, which can impact consumer spending patterns.

- The value of a company's brand can also impact its investment potential.

CONCLUSION

"The most contrarian thing of all is not to oppose the crowd but to think for yourself."
— Peter Thiel

Mastering the art of fundamental analysis is a crucial step in becoming a successful investor. As you've already learned, it is a process that involves a deep understanding of assessing a company's value, reading financial and non-financial information, and having sound knowledge of its industry and market position and the overall economic environment. By using the tools and resources provided in this book, investors can become well-informed and confident in their investment decisions.

We started by introducing you to fundamental analysis and explaining its importance and role in investing. And then, we proceeded to discuss the different types of investments and, subsequently, the investment methods that use fundamental analysis. And all through until the end, we made sure not to leave any stone unturned.

One of the most important takeaways from this book is the significance of having a disciplined and patient mindset when investing. Successful investors such as Warren Buffett and Benjamin Graham have consistently emphasized the importance of these qualities.

To drive this point home, we can look at the success story of Warren Buffett's investment in Coca-Cola. In the 1980s, Coca-Cola faced stiff competition from PepsiCo, and its stock price declined. However, Buffett recognized the strength of the company's brand and the loyalty of its customers, and he invested heavily in the company. As a result, he realized a significant return on his investment.

So, you would agree that mastering fundamental analysis requires discipline, patience, and a willingness to learn and adapt continuously. By paying attention to a company's financial and non-financial information, industry and market position, and the overall economic environment, you can make informed decisions that lead to long-term success.

So, what next?

Of course, it's for you to go ahead and apply what you've learned to a real-world investment scenario. Now that you've finished reading this book, you're armed with the necessary tools and knowledge to conduct your own fundamental analysis.

Start by identifying a company you're interested in investing in, then work through each of the steps outlined in this book to evaluate the company's qualitative and quantitative factors and determine its intrinsic value. And in case you need help figuring out where to start, consider joining an online community of investors or contacting a financial advisor for guidance. Remember, the key to successful investing is always to continue learning and staying up-to-date with the latest developments in the market.

Meanwhile, I would greatly appreciate it if you could take some time to leave a review on Amazon with your feedback on the book.

I wish you good luck on your trading and investing journey.

Brian Hale

REFERENCES

Aguila, L. A. (2014, April 24). *Looking at corporate governance from the investor's perspective.* https://corpgov.law.harvard.edu/2014/04/24/looking-at-corporate-governance-from-the-investors-perspective.

Ampulski, G. (2015, August 4). *A strong management team: the top driver of business value.* https://www.axial.net/forum/a-strong-management-team-the-top-driver-of-business-value.

Apiday Blog. (2023, February 16). *The concept of impact on social and environmental issues and its implication for companies.* https://www.apiday.com/blog-posts/the-concept-of-impact-on-social-and-environmental-issues-and-its-implication-for-companies.

Artzberger, W. (2022, May 15). *Avoid these 8 common investing mistakes.* https://www.investopedia.com/articles/stocks/07/beat_the_mistakes.asp.

BDC. (2023). *How to conduct a competitive analysis.* https://www.bdc.ca/en/articles-tools/marketing-sales-export/marketing/how-evaluate-competition.

Bakke, D. (2022, July 26). *The top 25 investing quotes of all time.* https://www.investopedia.com/financial-edge/0511/the-top-17-investing-quotes-of-all-time.aspx.

Beattie, A. (2013, February 13). *5 skills that traders need.* https://www.investopedia.com/articles/investing/091714/5-skills-traders-need.asp

CFI Team. (2022, November 26). *Industry analysis.* https://corporatefinanceinstitute.com/resources/management/industry-analysis-methods/

CFO Selections Team. (2020, March 23). *Financial projections and analysis considerations.* https://www.cfoselections.com/perspective/financial-projections-and-analysis-considerations.

Carlozo, L. (2017, March 14). *10 skills the best investors have.* https://money.usnews.com/investing/slideshows/10-skills-the-best-investors-have?slide=8.

Deepta, B. (2019, July, 18). *Fundamental analysis: macro factors.* https://www.gomarkets.com/en/articles/central-banks/fundamental-analysis-macro-factors/

Dumont, M. (2023). *Time management tips for financial professionals.* https://www.investopedia.com/articles/financial-careers/08/time-management-financial-career.asp.

El Issa, E. (2021, March 22). *Do you know what your investments are? Most Americans don't.* https://www.nerdwallet.com/article/investing/do-you-know-what-your-investments-are-most-americans-dont.

Elearnmarkets. (2022, October 21). *Fundamental analysis of company – importance, advantages & example.* https://www.elearnmarkets.com/blog/fundamental-analysis-of-company/#steps.

Fajasy. (2022, March 19). *How to evaluate a company's management team.* https://stablebread.com/how-to-evaluate-a-companys-management-team/

Fernando, J. (2022, August 10, 2022). *Discounted cash flow (DCF) explained with formula and examples.* https://www.investopedia.com/terms/d/dcf.asp.

FinGrad Academy. (2022, September 12). *What are the merits and demerits of fundamental analysis?* https://blog.joinfingrad.com/what-are-the-merits-and-demerits-of-fundamental-analysis/

Frankel, M. (2022, November 8). *How to research stocks.* https://www.fool.com/investing/how-to-invest/stocks/how-to-research-stocks/

Girsch-Bock, M. (2022, August 5). *What are financial projections and why do you need them?* https://www.fool.com/the-ascent/small-business/accounting/articles/financial-projections/

Hayes, A. (2020, December 30). *Factors to consider when evaluating company management.* https://www.investopedia.com/articles/02/062602.asp.

Howell, R. (2023). *Emotional intelligence: mastering the brain and mind.* https://www.mytradersstateofmind.com/emotional-intelligence---mastering-the-brain-and-mind-that-trade.html.

Hua, L. (2019, April 16*). 5 macro factors that affect the stock market.* https://fairmontequities.com/5-macro-factors-that-affect-the-stock-market/

Jacobi, L. (2022, July 26). *What is fundamental analysis?* https://www.benzinga.com/money/fundamental-analysis.

Jones, M. J., & Saad, L. (2023). *What percentage of Americans own stock?* https://news.gallup.com/poll/266807/percentage-americans-owns-stock.aspx.

Kennon, J. (2022, January 25). *The Basics of Income Statement Analysis.* https://www.thebalancemoney.com/investing-lesson-4-income-statement-analysis-357580.

Kenton, W. (2022, July 12). *Risk assessment definition, methods, qualitative vs. Quantitative.* https://www.investopedia.com/terms/r/risk-assessment.asp.

Muller, C. (2021, September 16). *The Pros and Cons of Socially Responsible Investing.* https://www.doughroller.net/investing/pros-and-cons-of-socially-responsible-investing.

Murphy, B. C. (2022, November 15). *Understanding the Cash Flow Statement.* https://www.investopedia.com/investing/what-is-a-cash-flow-statement/

O'Connor, M. (2023). *What is fundamental analysis in investing?* https://learn.wealthbase.com/what-is-fundamental-analysis-in-investing/

Paddle Blog. (2023). *7-step guide to financial forecasting & planning for any business.* https://www.paddle.com/resources/financial-forecasting.

Peterdy, K. (2022, November 28). *Corporate governance.* https://corporatefinanceinstitute.com/resources/esg/corporate-governance.

Powell, S. (2023, February 15). *Six essential skills of master traders.* https://corporatefinanceinstitute.com/resources/career/six-essential-skills-of-master-traders/

Price, N. J. (2019, August 19). *Why corporate governance is important to investors.* https://www.diligent.com/insights/shareholder-investor/why-corporate-governance-important-investors/

Ross, S. (2022, January 20). *The Main Focus Points When Analyzing a Balance Sheet.* https://www.investopedia.com/ask/answers/050615/what-items-balance-sheet-are-most-important-fundamental-analysis.asp.

Safdie, S. (2022, September 29). *Socially Responsible Investing (SRI): All you Need to Know.* https://greenly.earth/en-us/blog/ecology-news/socially-responsible-investing-sri-all-you-need-to-know.

Schmidt, J. (2023, February 19). *Stock valuation.* https://corporatefinanceinstitute.com/resources/valuation/stock-valuation/

Schwab. (2018, June 11). *Macro-economic factors of fundamental analysis.* https://www.cnbc.com/advertorial/2018/06/11/macro-economic-factors-of-fundamental-analysis.html.

Segal, T. (2022, August 25). *Fundamental analysis: principles, types, and how to use it.* https://www.investopedia.com/terms/f/fundamentalanalysis.asp

Swenson, S. (2022, June 28). *What is competitive advantage?* https://www.fool.com/investing/how-to-invest/stocks/competitive-advantage/

The Investopedia Team. (2022, August 30). *Warren Buffett's investment strategy.* https://www.investopedia.com/articles/01/071801.asp.

The Investopedia Team. (2022, September 03). *Intrinsic value defined and how it's determined in investing and business*. https://www.investopedia.com/terms/i/intrinsicvalue.asp.

Trexler, E. (2017, March 22). *Why successful investors focus on competitive advantages, not just profits*. https://www.forbes.com/sites/forbesfinancecouncil/2017/03/22/why-successful-investors-focus-on-competitive-advantages-not-just-profits/?sh=3acc6664e709.

Tuovila, A. (2022, September 21). *Forecasting: what it is, how it's used in business and investing*. https://www.investopedia.com/terms/f/forecasting.asp.

Wall Street Peep. (2023). *Relative value*. https://www.wallstreetprep.com/knowledge/relative-value.

Zhou, M. (2022, November 28). *ESG, SRI, and Impact Investing: What's the Difference?* https://www.investopedia.com/financial-advisor/esg-sri-impact-investing-explaining-difference-clients.

Zucchi, K. (2021, December 01). *Stock analysis: forecasting revenue and growth*. https://www.investopedia.com/articles/active-trading/022315/stock-analysis-forecasting-revenue-and-growth.asp.

THE LOVE OF THE GAME

Bradley Ambridge

"I couldn't settle in Italy - it was like living in a foreign country.'"
Ian Rush

"I would not be bothered if we lost every game as long as we won the league."
Mark Viduka

"We lost because we didn't win."
Ronaldo

"I faxed a transfer request to the club at the beginning of the week, but let me state that I don't want to leave Leicester."
Stan Collymore

"The first 90 minutes are the most important."
Bobby Robson

"Of the nine red cards this season we probably deserved half of them."
Arsene Wenger

Reporter to Gordon Strachan: "Gordon, can we have a quick word please?"
Strachan: "Velocity" [then walks off]

"Argentina won't be at Euro 2000 because they're from South America."
Kevin Keegan

"I spent a lot of my money on booze, birds and fast cards. The rest I just squandered."
George Best

"Some people think football is a matter of life and death. It is much more important than that."
Bill Shankly